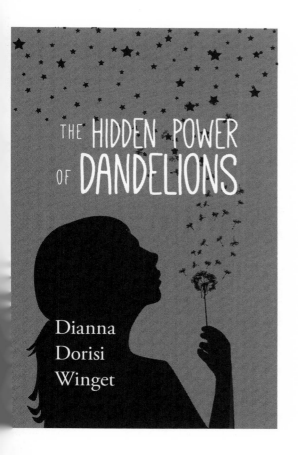

THE HIDDEN POWER OF DANDELIONS

Dianna
Dorisi
Winget

THe Hidden Power of Dandelions

Copyright © 2019 by Dianna Dorisi Winget

THE HIDDEN POWER OF DANDELIONS

CHAPTER ONE

I'VE HEARD THE human bite can generate 265 pounds of force, which is a drop in the bucket compared with what a lion can do, but it's still plenty enough to make my jaw burn as I watch Uncle Gus heave Dad from his wheelchair. It's not that I mean to clench my jaws, it just kind of happens when I see scary, unnatural stuff. And nothing's as unnatural as seeing your Dad get handled like a rag doll.

Uncle Gus groans with the effort of dead-lifting 170 pounds, while Mom yanks the wheelchair out of the way so he can ease Dad onto the bed. That's why we're here in Washington instead of back home in Oregon. Even Mom and I working together can't do what Uncle Gus now does several times a day.

I start to tug a sheet over Dad's skinny legs but he waves me away. "No, Rylee, I'm cooking as it is."

I jerk my hand back. "Okay, sorry, sorry."

"Drop the blinds," Dad says. "Maybe that'll help."

Mom nibbles her lip. It leaves the slightest smear of pink pearl lipstick on her teeth. "Are you sure, Mike? It's so pretty outside, wouldn't you rather have the light?"

"I'm sure," Dad snaps.

Uncle Gus raises his eyebrows at Mom and she offers a soft nod in reply. "Okie-doke," he says, allowing the mini-blinds to clatter down. "How's that, bro?"

"Better," Dad says.

But it's not better. It's like he's decided to slink off into some dark, gloomy cave. And in all my twelve years, I've never seen Dad slink off from anything. It makes my heart feel like it's being squashed. I grab the TV remote and offer it to Dad. "Seahawks are playing."

"Not now," he says. "I just wanna rest."

The worst part is, I can't tell if he's turning down the game itself, or watching it with me. I drop the remote on his bedside table. "Well … in case you want it later," I say, before escaping out the sliding glass door to the back yard.

The hot rush of sunshine is like a welcome hug, but I still have a crushy, cold sweat sensation on the inside. A school nurse once told me that even though anxiety doesn't feel good, it's a temporary and normal response to stress. But I'm not so sure my body's normal. It's great at amping up, but real lousy at calming down. I'm wishing I had a squeezie ball right now, but Mom doesn't know I'm using them again, so I drop down on the porch steps and take several deep breaths instead.

Compared to Oregon's salty moisture the air here in Cayuse is as dry and raspy as sandpaper. It leaves a roughness on the back of my throat, my hands, and on my lips. At least it makes the fruit trees happy. Cayuse is called the fruit bowl of the nation, and Uncle Gus says the air smells like whatever crop is being harvested. Last month, he says the whole valley smelled like a ripe peach. Now that it's late September, the air smells like a Concord grape—sweet on the inside, lip puckery on the out.

Coco naps in the shade of the garden shed, her pudgy paws stacked on top of each other. "Hey, girl," I call over the roar of the air conditioner, and she bounds up like I've shaken a bowl of kibble in her ear.

She scrambles into my lap and I kiss the white stripe running down her stubby, wrinkled muzzle before she soaks my chin with sloppy kisses. Then she plunks her head down against my collarbone like she thinks I'm the best, most trustworthy person in the whole world. I'm not. Not even close. But Coco's trust is so true and wonderful I quit breathing in hopes she won't move. About ten heartbeats later the patio door slides open and her tail starts drumming. I fake scowl at Uncle Gus. "Aww, man, you woke her up."

Coco wiggles out of my arms and takes a zigzag lap around the yard. Then she comes back and wedges herself between me and the neglected wooden ramp Uncle Gus built for Dad. Dad's wheelchair has rolled across it exactly once in the three weeks we've been here—the first day, when Uncle Gus pushed him from the car to the house. Since then he's hidden indoors, tucked inside his own shell like the little turtles Molly and I used to play with at Talache slough. And even though it's not fair to be upset with him over something not his fault, I still am. He should come outside. It would make him feel better.

Uncle Gus lowers himself onto the step beside me. "Hey, there, Private, how goes the battle?"

I give him a playful punch to the shoulder. "At this moment, sir, I'm afraid the outcome is uncertain."

He smiles and drapes a heavy arm around me. "Yep, I know what you mean." He's dressed in his blues from the fire station and smells like a burnt marshmallow. Dad always used to smell like that too, like warmth and safety. Now he reeks of alcohol wipes and metal like a hospital. I try hard not to wrinkle my nose around him because I know it's rude and might hurt his feelings, but sometimes I catch myself too late.

The tinny roar of a crowd seeps through the open slider. Dad's watching the game after all. My nose stings, and I talk fast so I don't cry. "Hey, Uncle Gus, do you have a blender? I need to make Dad one of my famous banana smoothies."

He drags a thumb over his moustache, looking embarrassed. "Afraid I don't. Smoothies sound … awfully healthy."

I grin. "You can make unhealthy things with a blender too, y'know? Milk shakes, cake batter, all kinds of bad for you stuff."

He brightens. "Oh, well in that case."

A blue butterfly flits around the daisies at the edge of the yard, folding and unfolding its wings like it's just learning to use them. Something about its fragile beauty makes me sad again. "Sure wish Dad would come out here."

"He will," Uncle Gus says. "I'll have him out here mowing my dandelions in no time."

His words startle me a little because they bring to mind such a clear picture of Dad doing that very thing. We're back in Oregon, and Dad's wearing black running shorts, bobbing his head to the beat of the music from his earbuds as he plows down the crop of dandelions Mom's upset about.

When I was little, I used to cry when their happy yellow faces disappeared under the angry growl of the mower. But one day Dad whispered in my ear not to worry, that dandelions possessed hidden powers that enabled them to come back bigger and stronger after they were mowed. Just watch and I'd see. So I did watch, and he was right. Two days later they were back—bigger, stronger, and happy as ever. That's when dandelions became my favorite flower. When I'm scared to do something, I tell myself I have hidden powers too. Sometimes it helps.

I tip my head against Uncle Gus's shoulder. "Do you think Dad will ever be the same again?"

He doesn't sigh out loud, but I feel his shoulders rise and collapse a few seconds later. "Not the same, no. But he'll still be your dad, and he'll still love you. We have to give him time."

I know it's supposed to comfort me, but it's the same frustrating bologna the doctors keep feeding us. *Don't expect too much too soon. Losing your mobility is similar to any other tragic loss. Each patient has to work through the grieving process at his own pace. Yada, Yada, Yada.* The only person they ever talk about is Dad. But Mom and I are grieving too. Dad still has us, but we don't have him. Not the same him, anyway. How come the doctors never talk about us?

My chest muscles are squeezing hard again, and I reach over to pet Coco until they loosen a little. She raises her head and pulls her lips back over her top teeth.

"Whoa," Uncle Gus says.

I giggle. "It's okay, she's just smiling." And I'm tickled he doesn't know this, because I love that she smiles only for me.

He cocks an eyebrow. "Goofy dog. I'm afraid nobody's gonna claim the little mutt. We haven't gotten any calls from the poster at the firehouse."

I pop upright with sweaty palms. I've been preparing for this conversation for the past week, but now that it's suddenly here I'm not ready. "What are you gonna do with her?"

"Take her to the shelter, I guess. I should've made Hernando take her home, he's the one who brought her in to the firehouse."

"He doesn't want her?"

"His kid's got allergies."

"Oh." I gaze into Coco's chocolate eyes and get all quivery with panic. "Well, you better wait a little longer. Somebody might still claim her."

"Yeah, I guess a few more days won't hurt."

I gather a big breath for courage and then slap my knee like I've just solved one of the world's great riddles. "Or ... wait," I say. "I've got it. You could keep her yourself."

Uncle Gus snorts. "Keep her? I don't have time for a dog."

"I do. I could help take care of her."

"Whoa now, hold on Rylee. Dogs are a lot of work. And I think you've got a pretty full plate already, going to school and helping your mom."

My throat starts to narrow and I pinch the underside of my leg as a distraction. He's right, of course. Mom does depend on me way more now than before Dad's accident. But I could never be too busy for Coco. She's the best squeezie ball ever invented. Even in daytime she keeps me grounded. But I need her most at night, when thoughts of Molly barrel through my mind like a freight train, and the guilt threatens to derail me. But when I hug Coco close enough to feel her warm little puffs of breath on my cheek, and the way her heartbeat pats my arm, somehow I manage to stay on track.

Even if I tried to explain, Uncle Gus wouldn't get it. He's the most stable person I know. I'd sound ridiculous.

I'd probably cry. No, this is one of those times that calls for some good, old-fashioned begging, no matter how pathetic and babyish it might make me sound. I meet him eye to eye. "I really want to keep her," I say. "Please, please, please."

Uncle Gus is six feet tall and stocky, but he jerks back with a scaredy-cat expression. "But your mom doesn't even like dogs."

His face makes me want to laugh, but this is too serious of a situation so I rein it in. "Sure she does," I say. "Just not little dogs, like the yappy Poms she grew up with."

"Um ... I still think that's something you'd need to run past your parents."

I shrug. "Why? It's your house. Besides, I already named her."

"You did?"

"Yeah, Coco, because her eyes are the color of hot chocolate. Check 'em out. It's perfect, right?"

He grimaces. "Hey, kiddo, gimme a break here, because the last thing I want is to tell you no. But I'm not sure your ..."

My insides are jumping and popping like a fried egg, and I have an overwhelming urge to move. I grab one of Uncle Gus's meaty hands with both of mine and raise it to my forehead like some helpless damsel in desperate need of rescue. I've been around firefighters all my life. I know that most of them are suckers for people in need. "Just wait. Here's the thing, okay? If you let me keep her, I promise to teach her something useful to a fireman."

My own words surprise me so much I drop Uncle Gus's hand. Finding a way to get Dad back into firefighting is pretty much all I've thought about since his accident. But it's a deep, closely guarded secret. And I can't believe how close I just came to blurting it out.

Uncle Gus is waiting, the corners of his eyes crinkled. "No kidding? I'm listening."

I recover fast and do my best to look smug. "Um ... okay, so I don't know right at this moment what that might be, but she's smart, she could learn anything. Look at her."

Coco jumps to her feet and bows low, her butt swaying in the air, like being stared at is an invitation to some new game. We both laugh. "Not sure I'm seeing smart," Uncle Gus says. "All I see is goofy."

"Trust me," I say. "I'll come up with something good, I swear."

"Something useful to a fireman, huh?"

"Yes," I say. "Plus, I'll feed her and take care of her and pick up her poop, and do whatever else she needs. Pleeeeease, Uncle Gus."

He slaps his forehead. "Aye-Yai-Yai."

"Sounds like a yes to me." I hold out my fist, and he studies it for a few seconds before bumping it with his own.

"Okay," he says, "tell you what. We'll try it for a few weeks. But if your folks have any problem with it then she's gonna have to go to the shelter. Fair enough?"

I punch the air. "Yesssssss! Thank you."

His pager buzzes and he grabs it off his belt loop as he stands. "Gotta get back to the station. Later, gator."

I offer a mock salute and wait for the slider to close before collapsing against the steps. I'm lightheaded and weak, but I manage to drag Coco onto my lap and squeeze her tight. "OMG, Coco! Do you get what just happened here? I saved you from the shelter. Now it's your turn to help save me, okay? We have to convince Dad he can still be a fireman. Think we can do it, girl?"

Coco flattens her ears and wiggles all over. And even though I know I should be thrilled, my heart is racing and my teeth are chattery with fear, because she has absolutely no idea I'm asking the impossible.

CHAPTER TWO

I CART COCO BACK inside and over to Dad's bed. He's watching a rerun of L.A. Firefighters, but he flips the channel like he doesn't want me to know. It shatters a little piece of my heart that he doesn't want to share it with me anymore. I used to get such a kick out of watching each episode with him, listening to him analyze which parts were real and which ones were pure Hollywood. I clear my throat. "What happened to the Seahawks?"

He swats the air. "It was a lame game."

"Oh. Well, guess what, Dad? Nobody claimed Coco so Uncle Gus decided to keep her. Isn't that the best thing since whipped cream?" I rock back and forth as Dad turns cool eyes on Coco. But then he smiles and says, "Not sure I'd go that far, but she's cute enough. Looks like she's got a lot of beagle in her."

11

"I think so too. But her face is kind of wrinkly like a pug. I think she may be a puggle." I giggle as I say it, because who can say puggle with a straight face?

"Mmm," Dad says. "I can't picture Gus having time for a dog."

"Yeah, well, I offered to help with her. I don't mind."

He takes her from my arms and rubs her ears. "Hey, pup. What are you good for, huh? Probably not much." Coco gnaws his knuckle and he picks up his rubber hand grip and offers it to her instead.

I wince and glance over my shoulder, expecting Mom to swoop in and remind us about how much everything costs. "Um … aren't you supposed to be using that for therapy?"

"Aw, it's worthless," Dad says. "Let her chew it up."

"I'm gonna teach her to do stuff," I say. "What do you think I should start with?"

"Teach her not to pee in the house."

I giggle again, which is the most Dad has made me laugh in weeks. "She already knows that."

"What kind of stuff then?"

I consider my words. Dad seems a little more like himself for the moment. Would it be okay to share just a little of my plan? "Something to help a fireman. Got any good ideas?"

Dad frowns. Then he raises his blue eyes to mine, and it's a little like peeking through the window of an abandoned home that used to be full and happy. "Better ask your uncle," he says. "He's the only fireman in the family now."

My heart seizes a little, and part of me wants to blurt out that I'm going to fix everything for him, I've got it all figured out. But I know better, because the truth is, I really don't have anything figured out ... not yet, anyway. "Don't say that Dad. You'll always be a fireman."

He closes his eyes briefly before giving me a tight-lipped smile, and I see I've lost him again. "Take your pup, Rylee. She's hurting my stomach."

"Oh, okay, sorry." I scoop Coco into my arms and twist the hand grip until she lets go. I should just leave, but I have to try one more time. "Do you wanna play a game or something? Scrabble, maybe?"

Dad clears his throat. "Maybe later, okay? Think I'll watch TV for now."

"Sure," I say, and try to smile even though it's the last thing I feel like doing. "But keep thinking about what I can teach Coco, okay?"

"Will do," he says, flatly, and it's clear I'm dismissed.

I head down the hall and try to prepare myself for the really scary part—telling Mom about Coco. She could ruin everything. But there's no sense procrastinating, because the longer I wait, the sicker my stomach will get. I follow the mumble of Mom's voice to the closed door of her bedroom. It only takes a moment of eavesdropping to learn she's on the phone with some insurance person, and I know not to interrupt. I hover for a few more seconds until Coco distracts me with a grumbly snort.

"What, silly girl?" I say, glancing down, and she flattens her ears and licks her lips like she's apologizing for the interruption. I move across the hallway to my bedroom. Uncle Gus's weight bench and treadmill are shoved against the far wall, creating a narrow path in between the stack of boxes still waiting to be unpacked. My old bed won't fit, but I don't mind sleeping on an air mattress. It's cool actually, kinda like camping without the mosquitoes.

I grab my story notebook off the floor and take Coco back outside to wait until Mom's free. We play tug of war with an old sock until she collapses into a panting heap at my feet. Then I sink into a lawn chair, open my notebook and reread the last few pages of my fantasy novel. My main character, Anastar, has discovered the rebel luminary base where her mom's being held captive. But she has only twenty four hours to free her before the Illusionist makes the captives disappear forever.

I sigh. I've been stuck at this point ever since Dad's accident when I lost touch with the Wednesday Warriors. That's what our librarian, Mrs. D, called our little writing group back home. We met for two hours every Wednesday after school to write, eat snacks and compare notes on whatever book of the month we'd chosen. It was my favorite two hours of the whole week.

But now, without the Wednesday Warriors, my creative juices are all thick and sludgy. I've done what the writing books say to do, plunge my main character into a crisis. That part was easy. But I have no idea how to get Anastar out of the mess she's in, or how to help her rescue her mom. The books don't tell you how to do that.

I flip to a blank page and start doodling random shapes, but it's only seconds before thoughts of Molly needle their way in, every bit as painful as the flu shot Mom makes me get each winter. I've deleted her photos from my phone, ignored her texts and blocked her on social media. But my brain doesn't have a delete button. And it doesn't seem to get that I don't want to think about Molly, that we can never be friends again. It refuses to trash six years of memories. I rip the page free, crumple it and toss it a pitiful three feet. Stupid, worthless paper.

"Rylee," Mom says.

I jump, wondering why I didn't hear the slider open. "Oh, hey," I say.

Coco's a few feet away, making soft slurping noises in her sleep, and Mom studies her for a moment as she drags over a lawn chair. "I hear Gus says she can stay."

I catch my breath and try to read Mom's expression. When she's happy, her face is all bright and glowy like a full moon. But if she's angry, she's all dark and closed up like black construction paper. Right now she's somewhere in the middle, which is totally unnerving. "Did you know beagles are considered mid-size dogs?" I blurt. "They don't bark much either. Hardly ever," I add, though I have no idea if this is true or not.

Mom doesn't respond. She sits with purpose, crosses her legs and regards me with an expression that's gone grouchy. "Did you have anything to do with your uncle's decision?"

"What? No!"

"Well, the name Coco doesn't strike me as something he'd come up with."

"It doesn't? What would he name her?"

"Oh, I don't know. Maybe Dog, or Fido, or something unoriginal like that."

The fact that she sounds more tired than angry fills me with hopeful energy, and I allow a smile to slip out. "Okay, so maybe I did pick her name. But Uncle Gus is still the one who decided to keep her."

"Mm-hmm," she says, like she's convinced I'm full of bologna. "Well, I just don't see how it's gonna work."

I pinch the underside of my leg. "How what's going to work?"

"A dog," Mom says, sounding exasperated. "Gus is going on the early shift the next few weeks, and Lord knows I've got enough to take care of with your dad."

"Oh, Coco won't be any problem," I say. "She can stay outside while I'm at school, and I'll make sure she has what she needs before I leave in the morning. You won't have to do anything."

16

Mom makes a stutter of disapproval in the back of her throat, and I brace for the next argument, but she surprises me by not saying anything. Instead, she leans forward and clasps her hands around her slim legs. "Speaking of school, is lunch going better?"

I'm still wound tight, so it takes me a minute to loosen up enough to register the question. "Lunch?"

"Yeah. Did you find someone to sit with?"

"Oooh," I say. She's asking if anyone's invited me to join their table in the lunch room. No one has, and I don't want them to. But I can't admit that. I can't tell her how terrifying middle school cafeterias really are, the way everyone sits around casting suspicious glances at each other, like they expect a sniper attack at any moment. How the very idea of being trapped in such a loud, crowded room leaves me drenched in chilling sweat, a hair away from throwing up—as bad as the anxiety I suffered as a little kid. Back when I always kept a clean shirt in my backpack. But she doesn't need to know my fear is back. She has plenty enough to worry about already. I force a smile. "I'm not looking for anybody to hang with, Mom. I like sitting outside."

"All alone?"

"Yeah, all alone. There's this cool stone bench right by the library where it's quiet and shady and nobody bugs me."

She nibbles her lip. "Okay. Well, I found you something. In case you want it." She produces a plastic sack from behind her and pulls out a green silk scarf with fringes. "I found it at a thrift store yesterday and thought you might like it. Didn't you say a lot of the girls wear them here?"

I nod. It's true, scarves are super popular here, which is downright ridiculous since it's so warm. All the girls wear them in perfect loops around their neck or draped over their shoulders. I don't really care what the other girls are wearing, but Mom's heart is in the right place. I gently finger the scarf's fringes. "It's pretty. Thanks."

"You're welcome," she says. "I thought it might go really nice with that green T-shirt you've got. You know, the one with the cat on it?"

"It's a puma," I correct. "But yeah, okay. Maybe I'll wear it tomorrow." I fold the scarf into thirds, the same way Dad used to fold his work pants. "Did you know Uncle Gus doesn't have a blender?"

"I hadn't noticed."

"We need to get one," I say. "I need to make Dad a banana smoothie."

Mom breaks into a soft smile. "Always thinking about your dad, aren't you? He doesn't know how lucky he is."

I gawk at her. "Did you just say lucky? Bet he'd never use that word."

"I know," she says. "That's what I meant."

I'm not sure how to respond, because she's making as much sense as tree bark. "Do you know he doesn't think of himself as a fireman anymore?"

"That's sad," she says, "because it's all he's ever been in the seventeen years I've known him." She lets out a long sigh before she reaches over and starts massaging my neck. "Honey, Karen called earlier today."

I immediately sense a trap, and the air between us turns as cold and sharp as an icicle. "Why?"

"Just to check on Dad. She says Molly's pretty miserable."

"Good," I say. "She should be."

"Karen was wondering if maybe you might consider . . ."

"No," I say, pulling away. "No, I won't."

Mom's hand falls as I jump up. "Rylee, honey, I understand, believe me. That's why I haven't pushed the issue. But she's your best friend."

"*Was* my best friend."

"Fine," Mom says, sighing. "But don't you think you should at least hear her side of it?"

"I tried, remember? I begged her to talk to me and she wouldn't say a word."

"I know. I just think sometimes . . . well, people need second chances. And whether you agree or not, at some point you're gonna have to confront this thing."

"I will," I say. "At some point ten years from now, or maybe twenty."

"Rylee, stop."

My eyes prick with tears as I scoop up my notebook. "Thank you for the scarf," I say, heading for the porch. "I've got some homework to finish for tomorrow."

I glance at Dad on my way through the living room. He's dozed off with the remote in his hand, a week's growth of beard partially hiding his face. His arms are still tan below the white sleeves of his T-shirt, his legs splayed at an odd angle like a twisted grasshopper. Just a few short months back he helped his crew finish second in a regional Stair Climb competition by racing up 60 flights of stairs—wearing 50 pounds of bunker gear, no less—in 14 minutes flat. Who'd ever believe that now? Nobody, that's who. If I hadn't seen it with my own eyes, I wouldn't either.

Now his whole life is on a stupid bedside table—water pitcher, phone, pills, liniment for bed sores, his therapy schedule, the tinny bell he uses to signal us if we aren't nearby. Lucky? I can't believe Mom actually used that word. Miserable is more like it. And seeing him like that makes me miserable too. Worse than miserable, really. It makes me want to kick and smash something and scream and cry, all at the same time. Because about seventy five percent of what happened to him is Molly's fault ... but the remaining quarter?

Well, let's just say that sometimes I hate myself almost as much as I hate her.

CHAPTER THREE

THE DAY WE *meet we are both wearing white sneakers with red lights that flash when we jump or run. We're at the community appreciation picnic for first responders and I'm starving. The food table stretches out like a glorious slip-n-slide, and the chocolate brownies are screaming my name. But the mayor keeps blabbing on and on about how much we all owe to the Elliott Bay police officers and firefighters and Mom refuses to let go of my hand.*

I'm two seconds from a meltdown when I catch sight of you crouching in the shadow of the gazebo. Then you step out into the sun, and I see your hair is as shiny as a black stone under water. Creeping, creeping so your shoes don't light up, you duck under the checkered red plastic table cloth. I hold my breath and wait until your hand shoots up and makes a grab for a piece of fried chicken. Only you grab too hard, and instead of one piece, the whole tub spills across the table.

I laugh out loud and everyone turns to look. Too late, I realize my mistake. Your mom rushes over with a face as red as sliced watermelon. She rights the tub and studies the chicken like she's not sure what to do with it before gathering it all up and dropping it back in the bucket. Then she swats your bottom. But you don't cry. I'm so impressed with your bravery.

I'm sure you must hate me for ratting you out. But amazingly, you don't. After we finally get to eat, you join me in a patch of dirt under a birch tree and we make a worm condo by mounding up a small hill of earth and decorating it with moss and sticks and birch bark. After we get bored, we run with our arms circling like windmills until we fall down in the grass, dizzy and laughing, like we've been best friends forever.

CHAPTER FOUR

I SIT CROSS-LEGGED ON the stone bench outside the library, sipping apple juice and people watching behind the safety of my phone. I tug my scarf away from my throat. The fringes tickle like spider legs, and the extra material makes me feel like a mummy in the afternoon warmth. Still, Mom's big, goofy smile this morning was worth it. I haven't seen that smile near enough lately.

A burst of squealing explodes a few yards away. Two girls are crouched near the door to the sixth grade wing, their foreheads almost touching. It rubs the sore place inside me because it reminds me so much of Molly and me. The girls even look a little like us—one has my straggly, cider colored hair, and the other has Molly's glossy, untamed curls. But it's definitely not us. Our friendship is three months and three hundred miles in the past. It will never be us again.

I focus back on my phone and the 161,000 puppy training videos on YouTube. It's amazing what a dog can learn beyond the sit, stay and shake hands kind of stuff. Some can sniff out cancer, detect smuggled rhino horn or ivory, or play professional Frisbee. It fills me with hope, because if they can do all that, surely they can learn something useful to a fireman. I try Googling *fire station dogs*, but the only articles that pop up are about Dalmatians who do nothing besides ride along in the truck.

A blur of motion catches my eye and I glance over to see Mrs. Foxworthy taping a yellow poster to the door of the library. I wait until she disappears back inside and then slip over for a closer look.

YOUNG AUTHORS WANTED

Submit a short story, article or novel chapter to our young authors writing competition. The three highest scoring entries in each category will receive a cash prize, publication in the Cayuse County Times, plus free admittance to our Young Authors Boot camp to be held at the end of the year, presented by famed Washington novelist Sabrina Seoung. See Mrs. Foxworthy for details!

I nibble my fingernail as adrenalin spurts through me. Sabrina Seoung! She writes the kind of books I want to write—fantasies that transport you to other worlds where you don't have to worry about real life problems smacking you in the face—stories that set you free. Taking a workshop with her would rate as high on the coolness scale as teaching Coco to do four pawed back flips. Not that backflips would help a fireman, but I bet Coco would love them anyway. I can just see her joyful look, her jowls hanging loose, spotted belly turned up to the sun.

The image makes me giggle, but then reality slaps me in the head and the image fades. I can't even finish my book, much less make it contest worthy. What a joke. But my feet carry me right through the door to the library anyway.

I'm relieved to see the chunky wooden tables in the foyer are mostly empty. Mrs. Foxworthy smiles at me from behind a humming copy machine. "Good afternoon."

"Hi," I mumble, trying not to stare at the large gap between her front teeth. "I was wondering if I could get more information about the writing contest."

Her grin nearly splits her round face in two. "Ohhh, I just posted that. Are you a writer?"

She's not exactly yelling, but it feels like it, and heat rushes my face. I inch closer in hopes she might lower her voice. "Um … yeah, sort of."

"Wonderful. Remind me of your name, dear."

"Rylee. Rylee Willet."

"So what do you like to write, Rylee?"

"Fantasy mostly."

She puts a hand over her heart and leans toward me. "Oooooh, fantasy. How exciting." She opens a folder on her desk, pulls out three sheets of paper and gives them a crack with the stapler. "Here you are, everything you need. Read it over and let me know if you have any questions. I hope you enter. It's such a marvelous opportunity."

"Okay, thanks." I roll the papers into a tube just before turning and colliding with someone right behind me. There's a loud "oomph" from both of us. Then my startled brain recognizes the black hair and wire framed glasses. Miguel from science class. The boy who loaned me a pen the other day.

He jumps back with a twisty step. "Whoa, sorry!"

I skirt around him in a panic. "Yeah, me too."

"Rylee, wait," Mrs. Foxworthy says. "Do you know Miguel? He's a writer too."

My chest clamps down and I struggle to breathe. Girls are scary enough to talk to, boys are a hundred times worse. But I've only made it a few feet, not nearly far enough to pretend I didn't hear. I jam my hand into my pocket and close my fingers around my squeezie ball before turning around. "Um … yeah, we have science together. Hey, Miguel."

He wiggles his fingers at me. "So what do you like to write?"

The question floats in the air a few seconds before hardening into a big dry lump, like Play-Doh left out too long. What do I like to write? What's writing? But then I notice his Seahawks jersey and I relax a little. "Fantasy," I say. "How 'bout you?"

He bumps up his glasses. "Short stories mostly, about sports and outdoor stuff."

"Nice."

Mrs. Foxworthy beams, like she's brought together two accomplished celebrities and is about to win the Nobel for it.

"Are you gonna enter the contest?" Miguel asks.

I shrug. "Um, probably not, maybe," I say, figuring it's safest to cover all your bases at once.

"You have something already written?"

"Kind of. I'm working on a book, but it's not even close to being done. I've been stuck lately."

"It doesn't have to be finished," Mrs. Foxworthy says. "You can enter a chapter."

"I might," I mumble. "I'll think about it."

Miguel's gaze drops to the hand I have shoved in my pocket, and my fingers freeze. If he didn't think I was weird before, he must now. The bell buzzes a few seconds later and I've never been more relieved. "Better go," I say. "Thanks, Mrs. Foxworthy."

I hustle out the door and take deep gulps until my chest starts to loosen. It's the first time I've ever talked to Miguel, except to mutter "thanks" when he loaned me the pen. He's quiet and nice and kind of cute too. Part of me hopes he doesn't try to talk to me again ... but part of me hopes he does.

I push the scary encounter out of my mind until I walk into science class two hours later and see Miguel talking to our teacher. My palms get all drippy, like I've dunked them in a bucket of saliva. I angle away as I pass Mr. Hinkle's desk and slip into my chair.

Mr. Hinkle tells everyone to find their seats. Then he starts lecturing about solids, liquids and gasses, and how matter can change from one state to another. I force myself to listen for the first few minutes, but it's not long before I start watching the clock, counting down the minutes until I can go home. It's 2:10, which means Dad's physical therapist, Roy, is probably at the house, or maybe his occupational therapist, Diane. Diane makes me nervous because she doesn't smile much, but Roy is great.

I love how he keeps up a steady stream of conversation, all encouraging and cheerful as he works Dad's joints and shows him how to use the trapeze bar above his bed to gain back upper body strength. And I especially love the way he reminds him it's possible for nerves to start working again if the spinal cord is only bruised or swollen. It's an elephant size *if*, for sure, but ... still. Roy manages to bring out a little of Dad's old sparkle. I wish he came every day.

Sudden laughter pulls my thoughts back to class. Mr. Hinkle is shaking his head and grinning. "No, Brian, that's not the kind of gas we're discussing."

I giggle, even though potty humor stopped being funny in third grade. But thirty seconds later my mind's back on Coco and how I can use her to help Dad. I'm not sure what in the world I was thinking when I made my promise to Uncle Gus. After all, some things naturally go together—peanut butter and jelly, waffles and syrup, world history and brain fog. But dogs and firefighting? And even if I can figure out a way to tie the two together, how's it supposed to make Dad strong and confident enough to believe he can still be a firefighter? How can it even begin to make up for the part I've played in ruining his life?

The dismissal bell finally rings and the room hums with twenty seven kids trying to beat each other out of class. "Pages thirty to thirty six," Mr. Hinkle calls. "Don't forget to read."

"So what part are you stuck on?" Miguel stands beside my desk, his camo bag slung over one shoulder, looking as relaxed as a tourist on the beach.

Anxiety sprouts in my chest like a weed. Our first conversation was tough enough. I'm not sure I can handle a second one. "Huh?"

Miguel bumps up his glasses. "Your book. In the library you said you were stuck some place."

"Oh." I manage a weak laugh. "Yeah, well... kinda toward the end."

"The climax? Those can be tough. Transitions are the hardest for me though."

I raise my eyebrows and he smiles. "My dad's a screenwriter."

This catches my attention, and for a minute I forget to be anxious. "Really? He writes for TV?"

"Yep. Ever watch Shadow's Alley? It's a cop show on cable. He writes a lot of those episodes."

"Cool."

Miguel beams. "Yeah, that's what I'm gonna do when I grow up. But I wanna do movie scripts. So what's your book about?"

Most of the kids have filed out, and the "tock-tock" of the big clock above Mr. Hinkle's desk suddenly sounds deafening. "You want to know right now?" I ask.

Miguel shrugs. "I walk," he says. "Do you have to catch the bus?"

My lungs refuse to expand all the way, and I feel woozy. "Noooo, but . . ."

"Cool." He grins and his eyebrows do a happy dance, like there's nothing else in the whole world he'd rather do than hear about my book. And I'm a little mystified and a lot terrified, because I've never had a boy pay me attention before. Well, not since kindergarten anyway, when Frankie Mills gave me a valentine professing his love for me, only to break my heart the next day by giving his *Hank the Cow Dog* bookmarker to another girl.

Silence vibrates between Miguel and me like a rubber band stretched to capacity. I'm breathless and feverish and have no clue what to say, but he waits patiently while I stuff my backpack, so I guess we're walking.

I stay several steps in the lead as Miguel and I thread our way through the hall and across the dry soccer field. Back in Elliott Bay, the grass grew lush and green, but here it's hard packed and clumpy, like it barely gets enough moisture to survive. I'm happy to see plenty of dandelions though, hiding their power behind sweet, golden smiles, and I focus on them instead of my hammering heart.

I glance at Miguel out of the corner of my eye, trying to identify the strange whistling sound he makes under his breath. Neither of us says a word until we've crossed the street in front of the school and started up the sidewalk on the other side. Miguel takes a quick side step to kick a rock. "So, you gonna tell me what your book's about now?"

I watch the stone bounce across the cracked cement and come to rest in the packed dirt at the base of a shade tree. "Um ... okay," I say. I make a show of clearing my throat. "It's about this girl named Anastar, and she and her mom live in this peaceful place called the Silver Barrows where nothing bad ever happens."

Miguel's brows wiggle and one shoots off to the side a bit. It's fascinating, actually. I wonder if he knows his brows can do that.

"You're staring at my eyebrows, aren't you?" he asks.

I gasp. "No I'm not!"

31

He laughs. "No problem. Everybody else does. I'm aware I have extremely gifted eyebrows. My Dad even named them—Calvin and Hobbes."

I slap a hand over my mouth as the laughter erupts. "Are you serious? The comic strip?"

"Yeah, Dad loves 'em. Anyway, back to your story. What keeps the peace in the Silver Barrows, some kind of magic?"

I shake my arms to get rid of nervous energy. "A special ring, actually. It's been passed down through the generations. But then one day, the ring gets stolen by this evil ruler of a nearby kingdom, his name's the Illusionist. And as soon as that happens, and the influence of the ring is gone, then chaos and unhappiness takes over the Silver Barrows."

Miguel's watching me, and it makes me self-conscious to have shared so much personal stuff with somebody I barely know. But he looks totally focused, so I decide maybe it's okay to say just a little more. "So anyway, Anastar's mom and a small group of villagers go on a quest to get the ring back."

"But they fail, at least at first."

I stop, surprised. "How do you know?"

"Because," he says with a smile, "as soon as they succeed, the story's over, right? So you can't make it too easy for them."

"I know that," I say, frowning. "Anyway, no, they don't get the ring back right away. They end up getting ambushed and kidnapped by the Illusionist. So Anastar has to go rescue them before the Illusionist makes them disappear forever."

"How long's she got?"

"Twenty four hours."

He whistles. "Not long. So what happens?"

"I'm not sure," I admit. "That's where I'm stuck."

"Hmm." Miguel looks lost in thought.

I speed to the lead again as we pass Dairy Depot, where a couple of sixth graders are hanging around with sodas. Miguel doesn't seem to notice.

"So who's Anastar's sidekick?" he asks a moment later, catching up.

"Her sidekick?"

"Yeah, who's her right hand man? All the famous heroes have one, you know? Tom Sawyer and Jim, Frodo and Sam, Huckleberry and Finn?"

"Oh." I nod meekly. "I see what you ... hey, wait a minute. Huckleberry and Finn?"

He flashes a sly grin. "Just wanted to see if you were listening."

I giggle. I can't help it.

"But no, for real," he says. "Who's Anastar's helper?"

I shrug, feeling like a total amateur. "She doesn't have one."

Miguel stops walking with an incredulous look. "Doesn't have one? Well, there's your problem right there."

I narrow my eyes. Part of me wants to ask him who he thinks he is, telling me how to write my own story, but another part of me is curious. "What do you mean?"

"I mean, you've given Anastar a herculean job with nobody to help her. She doesn't have anybody to bounce ideas off of, or to plan strategy with. She needs a best bud." He starts down the sidewalk again. "Everybody needs a best bud," he adds, more to himself than to me.

My jaw clenches and pain sears down my neck. Sidekick or helper? Maybe. But Anastar definitely does not need a best friend. Best friends are just that ... until they betray you. And when that happens, the pain is too great to be worth it. I hurry to catch up. "She doesn't need one," I say. "Anastar's really capable."

"Doesn't matter," Miguel says. "Even Superman needed Lois Lane."

All my muscles start to quiver, and I think I'll either burst into tears or punch him. He has no right to be so smug. He has no clue what I've been through. "Oh, yeah?" I demand. "So where's *your* best bud? Or doesn't anybody want to be friends with a know it all?"

Miguel winces like I kicked him, and I instantly regret my words. But I can't seem to stop myself from making it even worse. "You talk like you're some big, hot shot author," I say.

He raises his hands in surrender. "Jeez, sorry," he says. "I thought you wanted suggestions. But I guess you can figure it out by yourself."

My whole body is tingly and hot, and we've reached the corner of Third Street where I need to turn. "This is where I cut off," I say. "See you later."

Miguel gives a shrug. "Maybe," he says, the hurt clear in his voice.

I feel shaky and awful as he swings off the other direction. Part of me wants to call after him and apologize, try to convince him I'm not the jerk he thinks I am. But my tongue refuses to work, so I don't apologize. I don't say anything at all. Instead, I pull the squeezie ball from my pocket and smash the foam until it won't go any smaller. I keep it crushed the rest of the way home as I sort through my feelings about Miguel like so many canned goods, rejecting any that don't fit into the safe, cramped cage I've built around myself since Dad's accident.

Aside from the fact that Miguel thinks he knows everything, he's funny and surprisingly okay for a boy. He'd probably make a half way decent friend if I wanted one, but I don't. Friends are a lot like Fourth of July sparklers—pretty and fun at arm's length. But let them get too close, and they can leave you as blistered and raw as a third degree burn.

But then I consider it more and realize that Miguel doesn't have to be a *real* friend like Molly was. He can just be a *kinda* friend that stays on the surface and can't cause real harm—like a first degree burn that reddens your skin but doesn't go much deeper. The comparison makes me relax a little, because it means I don't have to be scared of Miguel. After all, he's nobody special, just some kid with ridiculous eyebrows in my science class who happens to like writing.

I'll never let him get close enough to hurt me.

CHAPTER FIVE

I
T IS YOUR *idea to rubber band our fingers. We are both eight years old and sitting on your bed when you bring over the two stretchy pink bands.*

"Let's see who can last the longest," you say. "It's so cool to see your finger go dead."

I don't think it sounds cool at all, but I think you're super cool, and I want to be like you. I let you loop the band around my thumb several times. It starts to throb after only a few seconds, but I try to be brave. "How long do we have to leave them on?" I ask.

"As long as you can stand it," you say.

You hop and skip around the room to distract yourself. But I hold still, biting my lip and trying not to cry. I tell myself I can do this—that I have secret powers like a dandelion. But then my thumb darkens from white to sickly gray to purple.

And suddenly I don't care who wins. All I want is to free my thumb. "You win," I say, as I struggle to tear off the band.

My blood rushes in with a horrible throbbing, like my thumb has a tiny heartbeat all its own. You pull off yours as well, and together we compare the deep grooves left in our skin. I feel so sorry for my thumb, for the damage I've caused it. And I'm almost panicked by the deep marks left behind.

"They'll go away soon," you promise.

But two hours later, when we shut off the light for bed, my thumb is still tender, and I can still see faint pink lines. It's the first time I realize how the pain we cause ourselves can sometimes last a long time.

CHAPTER SIX

I'M STILL THINKING about Miguel when I reach home. I step into the backyard and stop short. Dad's sitting in his wheelchair near the maple tree, wearing a baseball cap and sunglasses, waving a stuffed toy in front of Coco. Not only is he outside, he's playing with my dog—two super awesome things. "Whoa, Dad," I call, bouncing on my toes. "Look at you."

Coco bolts toward me, and I drop my backpack and scoop her into my arms. "Hey, baby, how's it going? You keeping Dad company?"

Dad folds his hands in his lap. "Hey, Rylee."

I free Coco and go over to hug him. "You came outside."

"Uh, huh. Your mom kicked us out."

I think he's kidding, but I'm not totally sure because I can't see if his eyes are crinkled at the corners. "Us?"

"Coco got into the kitchen garbage and strewed coffee grounds all over."

My insides turn to ice. "Oh, no. She was supposed to stay outside."

"She kept whining so your mom let her in. I think she got bored."

I have a new urge to grab my squeezie ball, but I don't want Dad to see. I scrunch the bottom of my T-shirt instead. "So . . . is Mom really mad at her?"

"Well, she wasn't a happy camper at the time, but I think she's over it. I offered to keep Coco busy out here for a while."

"Thank you," I breathe. And I'm not sure how to feel—worried that Mom's upset with Coco, or happy that it got Dad outside. I squat beside him and study the stuffed toy in his lap. "What is that?"

"An octopus. Not sure where it came from, but your pup already chewed two of its legs off." He dangles it between his knees, holding it just out of Coco's reach as she bounces up and down.

It gives me an idea. Maybe I can teach her to retrieve things for Dad. But no, he already has humans who can do that. Besides, he won't need that kind of help forever. Soon he'll be able to fetch his own stuff. "Think of anything I can teach her to help a fireman?"

Dad shakes his head with a puzzled smile. "What is it you think you're gonna teach her to do, Rylee? It's not like she can carry hoses or climb ladders. She's just a normal dog."

My face tingles with embarrassment. "Some dogs can climb ladders," I say. "I saw it on YouTube."

He smirks. "Oh, well, if it's on there, it's gotta be gospel truth."

His smirk makes my whole body sting, and I clench my jaw to keep from tearing up. Dad's never made fun of my ideas before. He says some of the world's greatest inventions spring from improbable ideas. But maybe he doesn't think that way anymore. Maybe the accident has changed more than just his body. Maybe it's also changed the way he views the world . . . and me. I struggle to swallow my hurt. "I promised Uncle Gus I'd teach her something useful," I say. "So that's what I have to do."

Dad nods, but he still looks skeptical, and I still want to cry. I focus on the nearest dandelion, two feet away. It's in danger of being decapitated by Coco's swinging tail, but it doesn't look a bit afraid. I pat my leg so Coco will move away. "So how was therapy with Roy today?"

"Grueling. How was your day?"

I think about my walk home with Miguel. "Grueling," I say.

Dad gives an unexpected chuckle, and it's like those first few seconds when your favorite song starts to play.

"How's the air mattress working out?" he asks.

"Fine. Pretty comfy actually."

"Not like your real bed though, huh?" Dad drops the octopus onto Coco's head and leans back in his chair, his smile gone. "I'm sorry about all this, Rylee. Taking you away from your home and your friends ... your life."

I duck my head. "It's not like any of this is your fault, Dad."

"Yeah." He reaches behind his sunglasses to rub his eyes. "But still ... thanks for being a trouper about everything." He clears his throat and nods at my backpack. "Looks like you've got some homework you should get to."

"Not much," I say "just some science. And a little math," I add, hoping he might take the bait. Dad's a total whiz at math, and he used to love helping me.

"Well, I'm getting thirsty," he says. "You mind grabbing me a glass of water?"

Disappointment crashes over me, just like the waves that used to swamp the rocks at Elliott Bay. "Yeah, sure," I say. But I hesitate a few seconds longer, trying to read his mind. Does he really want water, or does he just want me gone? And the fact that I can't tell makes me so sad. "Be right back."

My teeth ache as I trudge across the yard. I can't remember a time when Dad and I weren't close. Even our occasional disagreements never amount to much and are easy to fix, like slapping a Band-Aid on a papercut. But ever since the accident there's a strange distance between us, like we can be in the same room but still a mile apart. And I'm afraid they don't make a Band-Aid long enough to stick us together again.

I'm even more afraid he knows I had something to do with the accident, like he somehow senses it's partly my fault.

When I bring Dad's water back he's asleep, or pretending to be. I balance the glass on the lawn beside his chair and go back inside. I hug Mom and apologize for Coco spilling the garbage. She hugs me back, but doesn't say anything, which is not a good sign. Mom's not a yeller. With her, silence equals anger. I offer to take the garbage out to the bin by the curb, but she's already done it. So I offer to mop the floor, but she's already done that too. I can't think of anything else to do besides pray it won't happen again.

An hour later I'm in the kitchen doing science homework when Uncle Gus pushes through the door. "Hey, howdy," he says.

Mom straightens from unloading the dishwasher. "Oh, hey. I didn't think you were off for another few hours."

"I'm not," he says, "just making a pit stop." He swings a plastic grocery sack onto the counter and plunks another on the table in front of me. "For you," he says, winking.

I peek inside and squeal. "A blender! Cool. Now I can make dad his smoothie."

Mom's eyes go soft. "Oh, Gus, I didn't expect you to do that. I'll pay for it."

He flashes a good natured scowl. "You will not. If I want to buy my niece a blender, I'll buy her a blender. Besides," he adds, draping an arm around my shoulders, "she's gonna make me a smoothie too. A fattening, unhealthy one."

43

I giggle. "Only if you bought the right stuff."

"Guess you should check the other bag," he says.

I pop up from my chair to investigate. Bananas, orange juice, a carton of vanilla ice cream and a six pack of beer. I curl my lip. "I am not making you a beer smoothie, Uncle Gus."

He laughs. "The beer's not for that. Keep your grubby paws off it."

"No problem," I say. "Beer's disgusting."

Mom raises an eyebrow. "And you know this how?"

Uncle Gus grins.

"Dad gave me a sip once," I admit with a smile, and for a moment things almost seem normal again.

Uncle Gus messes up my hair and nods at Mom. "Mike's okay, right?"

"He's resting," she says.

"Okay, then, I'm off again. Gotta go see how Hernando's lasagna turned out." He tromps back out the door, pulling it closed behind him.

"Lasagna," Mom says with longing. "Sounds good, too bad it's so much work." She opens the fridge and gazes inside. "I guess we'll need something soon too."

"You don't have to cook," I say. "I'll make us smoothies."

"For dinner?"

I point at the ingredients. "Orange juice, fruit, dairy... completely balanced."

Mom eyes me with suspicion. "You normally use Greek yogurt, not ice cream."

"Aw, who cares, it all comes from fine bovines, right?" I clasp my hands together. "Please, Mom. I'm gonna make Dad the fanciest banana smoothie ever. It's gonna make him feel better. I know it is."

The doubt drains from her eyes and she gently cups my face in her hands. "I bet you're right."

I hum as I set up the blender, wash the jar and assemble my ingredients, including the two only Mom and I know about—a tablespoon of pancake syrup and a teaspoon of cinnamon. It's what elevates my smoothies to what Dad calls *legendary*. I float around the kitchen, picturing his happy surprise when I present it to him.

I've poured the creamy creation into a tall, chilled glass and piled it high with three inches of whipped cream when Dad lets out a yell. Mom tosses her dishrag and dashes into the living room. I drop the can of whipped cream and race after her.

Dad lays in the bed as straight as a steel rod, his fists clenched and his arm muscles corded like ropes.

"Spasms," Mom murmurs. And that one word is enough to make my stomach cramp. It happens at least once a week—the doctors call it dystonia. Dad says it's like a bad charley horse that refuses to let go. But I've never seen him this bad, and I stand helpless as he writhes and groans.

"We should call Uncle Gus," I say.

Mom shakes her head. "There's nothing he could do that we can't. Bring me a couple cold packs. Hurry."

I rush to the kitchen, glad for something to do. I bring two ice packs to Mom and she places one on each side of Dad's chest. Then she firmly begins massaging his right forearm and wrist. She ducks her head at me. "Get on his other side and help me, Rylee."

But I can't move. My own muscles are locked up like Dad's. "I can't," I whisper. "I don't know how."

"Do what I'm doing," Mom says.

I take a step back and shake my head. I've already hurt him enough. What if I make it worse?

Mom meets my eyes. "Rylee, I need your help. We have to relax his muscles. Please?" she adds.

I close my eyes. You can do this, I tell myself. You have to. Just be a dandelion. Then I skitter to Dad's other side, close both hands around his left arm and began squeezing and rubbing like Mom. "Do you think it's helping?" I ask after a few minutes.

"I think so," she says. "Keep going. Squeeze hard."

So I do, for as long as I can, until my fingers cramp and spasm. But I clench my jaw and make myself work through the agony. And there's something about the pain that's almost satisfying. After all, I deserve it. It's a small dose of justice for my part in putting him through this.

After what seems like forever, Dad's fists unclench and I risk a glance at his face. His panic has faded, and his eyes are closed.

Mom's bangs are damp, stuck against her forehead like they've been pasted on. "Finally," she whispers. "Finally." She shifts the ice packs to a different spot, and then we rub and stretch each of Dad's fingers until they lie flat. Dad's snoring by then and Mom lays his hand down on the mattress and motions me to do the same.

We tiptoe across the room and Mom gives me a smile. "Nice job," she whispers. "My arms feel like spaghetti, do yours?"

I nod. But the stress of it all closes off my throat and I can't speak. Mom opens her arms and I fall against her as the tears spill. "Hey," she says, wrapping me in a hug. "It's okay, baby. It's okay. You did great."

"But it's so unfair," I choke out. "He shouldn't have to go through stuff like that."

Mom shushes me gently. "Of course he shouldn't. But bad things happen to good people all the time. It's just life."

I shake my head as bitterness fills my stomach. "It's not life," I say. "It was Molly." *And me*, my conscience adds, but I don't say that part out loud.

Mom's breath is hot on the side of my head. "I know, honey. I know. And I'm sure she suffers for it every day." She lets me go and steps back. "Come on, let's get out of the living room and let Dad rest."

We round the corner into the kitchen and freeze.

Dad's smoothie. It's gone from a gorgeous pale yellow to a hideous brown. And the tower of whipped cream has melted, running down the glass in sticky, white trails that form a milky puddle on the counter. My perfect smoothie is ruined. I burst into a new round of tears. I've gone from a dandelion to limp lettuce.

"Oh, honey," Mom says. "I'm so sorry. Maybe you can blend it again later and it will still be okay."

"No," I say. "No, it won't. It's ruined. It's all ruined." I whirl away and storm down the hall, leaving Mom to clean up the mess. I know it's not right, none of this is her fault. But I'm so angry it's tough to breathe. I'm even mad at Coco when I see her sound asleep on top of my pajamas, her six legged octopus beside her. Why can't I be a dog? Not a stinking care in the world except for food and somebody to love you. I grab a squeezie ball and flop across the air mattress, but my fingers are too cramped to use the ball so I hurl it across the room instead. It whacks the candle sitting on my windowsill and releases a puff of vanilla into the air.

I glare at the ceiling for several minutes, huffing sighs and choking back my tears and disappointment. I wonder if what Mom said about Molly is true. If she really is suffering over what she's done? I hope so. Because I'm suffering, and she's a lot more to blame than me. I reach over Coco and retrieve my diary from my shirt drawer.

I haven't written any new entries for two weeks, but the urge to write one now is overpowering. I unclip the pen from the plastic spine, find a blank page and begin to write.

SEPTEMBER 22

Dad had bad spasms today. I helped Mom relax his muscles. It was so scary it made me want to puke. I can't explain what it's like to see your dad helpless and in pain. Dads are not supposed to be helpless. They are supposed to be strong. They are supposed to be the ones you go to when *you* feel helpless or scared. I wish I could trade places with him. Then he would still be the strong one.

I stare at my paragraph. I could write about the banana smoothie, but I suddenly don't have the heart or the energy to write anything more. I'm not sure where my anger went so fast, but now all I feel is flat and empty. I flip back to the beginning of the diary, scanning earlier entries, snapshots of the worst three months of my life.

JULY 6

Mom and I have been at the hospital for three days now. Dad's in a place called the ICU. He's hardly awake at all. The doctors say he has a severe spinal injury, but they aren't sure yet how bad. Grandma and Grandpa Russell flew in from Florida yesterday, and Uncle Gus is here too. All the guys from the fire station have been camping out with us in the waiting room. I want to hug Dad but I can't do anything but touch his hand. He's in a special bed with straps to keep him from moving. He has two needles stuck in his arm and sticky patches all over his chest so the doctors can monitor his heart. Grandma says I need to eat, but I'm pretty sure I forgot how.

JULY 14

Today we got both good news and bad. The good news is Dad's going to be okay. The bad news is he might never walk again. The scans show damage to a part of his lower spine called T-10. Mom can't stop crying. She says, how am I supposed to tell him? But I don't think she should tell him. I think the doctors are wrong. Dad will walk and run again. He has to. He's a fireman. The doctors don't know how strong he is.

JULY 21

The police came to the hospital to talk to us yesterday. They took Mom and me into a private room and told us more details about the car accident. They told us someone threw a football size rock off the overpass just as Dad drove under it on his way home. Then they told us they'd finished viewing the images from the freeway cam and did we want to see a photo of the only two people on the overpass around the time of...

I slap my diary shut hard enough to startle Coco. Her head snaps up and the fear in her eyes makes me melt. "I'm so sorry, girl," I whisper, pulling her close. "I didn't mean it." And I know those words are as much for me as they are her. Because even after three months, reading that diary entry is like taking a big breath under water.

Even with my eyes closed I can see every detail of the picture the police showed us—I see Molly's purple hoody, and the way her dark, glossy curls were trying to escape the polka dot scrunchie. I wanted so bad to believe the picture was some kind of trick, but then I saw Mom beside me, looking like a ghost, and I knew it wasn't a trick. That's when I ran into the bathroom and threw up.

There's no way Molly could ever... but she had.

Freeway cams do not lie.

CHAPTER SEVEN

I'M STILL IN my room an hour later when a rap sounds on my door. Coco jumps up as I cram the diary under my pillow. "Come in."

Uncle Gus pokes his head around the opened door. "Hey, howdy. It smells like dessert in here."

I gesture to the candle, which manages to scent the room with vanilla even when it's not lit.

"Ahh." He puts his hands on his hips and heaves a sigh. "Tough luck about the smoothie. Your mom told me."

"Yeah." I sit cross legged on my mattress and pull Coco onto my lap. I don't want to talk about the smoothie. All it will do is make me cry again.

Uncle Gus opens a folding chair and sits near me, and I breathe in his burnt marshmallow smell. "Got a proposition for you," he says. "Wanna come to the station tomorrow and wash trucks?"

Sadness seeps through me, and I'm not sure how to answer. Hanging out with Dad at the Elliot Bay station used to be my favorite way to spend a Saturday—washing trucks, teasing with the crew, sneaking cookies from the kitchen, and praying the alarm would sound because there's nothing in the world more exciting. Once in a while Dad even let me do a ride along. But now everything's changed, and the idea of going to the station with Uncle Gus feels wrong. Disloyal almost.

He studies my face. "Not something you have to do."

I wrap a hand around one of Coco's paws before asking the question that's haunted me for three months. "Uncle Gus, is there any way Dad can stay a fireman?"

The vibrating bass of a car stereo thumps through my open window, and Uncle Gus examines his ragged fingernails until the sound dies away. "Well, not in the traditional sense of handling hoses and ladders and putting out fires, no. But ... there's other aspects of being a firefighter."

I ponder his mysterious words. "Like?"

He casts a wary glance toward the door, and the hair on the back of my neck tingles. "Like education," he says, his voice low. "Public relations, that sort of thing."

"Education? You mean like teaching other firefighters?"

"Maybe. But I was thinking more like the public relations work we do for schools, community groups, you know."

And suddenly I get it, and my hands fly to my mouth. "Are you for real? You mean like teaching kids about fire safety and stuff?"

Uncle Gus is startled by my enthusiasm. He frowns and holds up a hand to hush me. "Hey, it's just something that crossed my mind."

But it's too late to hush me. I've already scooted Coco onto the mattress so I can bounce on my knees. "Dad could do that. He could totally do it."

"Maybe," Uncle Gus says. "But it would depend on a lot of things."

"Like what?"

"Like your Dad mostly. He'd still need to make a lot of improvement. Plus, he's such a hands on guy, I don't even know if he'd be interested."

I nod, but my heart is free-wheeling in my chest and I'm not even sure what he just said. All that matters is I'm not crazy. Dad *can* still be a firefighter. Uncle Gus has been thinking about it too. "Dad could so do that," I repeat. "He'd be perfect."

Uncle Gus raises his eyebrows. "It's a possibility. Let's leave it at that for now, shall we?"

"Yeah, sure," I say. Then my gaze falls on Coco and a jolt of energy shoots up my spine, because I've suddenly figured out how she can help Dad. I suck in a breath. "Ohmygosh!"

"What?"

"Nothing," I say, giggling. "But yes, I'll come wash fire trucks tomorrow, as long as Coco can come too."

He shrugs. "As long as you watch her."

I'm so lost in my own head I don't realize Uncle Gus has stood up and moved to the door. When I notice him again he's studying me with a puzzled expression. "What?" I ask.

He gives a slight shake of his head. "Just wondering, is all. Why is it such a huge deal your dad's a firefighter?"

The question knocks me from my happy place, and fills me with the stomach-dropping sensation of falling. "Well, b-because," I stammer, "you know it's the only way he'll ever be happy again."

Uncle Gus considers this a moment before nodding. "Yeah...maybe," he says. "Well, later gator."

I manage a nod as I wait for the door to close. Then I wilt onto the air mattress and bury my face in Coco's soft fur. It wasn't a lie. Dad *does* need to be a firefighter to be happy. And until he's happy again, I'll never be able to forgive myself. But there's more to it than just that. So much more.

It goes clear back to that magical day in third grade when I finally figured out who I was and where I belonged. When I discovered that Dad's identity as a firefighter, and my identity as his daughter, were interwoven as tightly as fibers in a rug. But the accident ripped those fibers apart, and I'm not sure who I am anymore. All I know is this—if I can't fix things for Dad soon, I'll slowly keep unravelling, just like those fibers, until I slip right back into that fearful, anxious little kid I used to be.

CHAPTER EIGHT

I T'S A THURSDAY *morning, six weeks into third grade, and my eyes are riveted to the clock. Dad's coming at nine thirty for show and tell and my whole body is humming like a happy bumblebee. I try not to show it. I glance at my spelling words and pretend to practice.*

Then comes a rap on our door and Dad steps into the room. He is decked out in full turnout gear and looks ten feet tall. All the kids stare wide eyed. I want to jump and dance and shout that this is my dad. But Mrs. White takes over for me. "Boys and girls," she says, "please welcome Captain Mike Willet, Rylee's dad."

Everybody gives me a quick glance, impressed and jealous, and I'm sure my face will melt right off I'm so proud. Dad catches my eye and winks.

There is lots of excited talking and laughing as the kids try on Dad's boots and hat and gloves, as they struggle to stay on their feet under the weight of the breathing tank. Then everyone gets quiet as Dad relates some of his near misses and rescues—especially his all-time favorite—when he saved old Mrs. Ripley's poodle from a house fire. I've heard this story a million times. But watching the faces of the kids as they listen now makes it seem new and more wonderful than ever. Mrs. White doesn't have to hush a single kid the whole twenty minutes Dad talks, and I feel happier and more relaxed than I have in ages.

But as amazing as Dad's visit is, what happens after he leaves is pure magic. Mrs. White assigns reading groups, and none of the kids lean away from me. No one teases me about my squeezie ball or tries to play keep away with it at recess. Instead, they ask me questions about Dad. Two of the kids say they want to be firefighters when they grow up.

And the next day, when everybody makes up kickball teams, I am the second kid picked. The second one. Let me tell you, that has never happened before. Not even close. I have been miraculously transformed from the weird, fun-to-pick-on kid, into the cool kid with the even cooler father. Dad's visit has somehow made them look at me differently. And for once, I'm not terrified the kids will laugh at me, or that I'll throw up at school in front of everyone. I don't even notice I've forgotten my squeezie ball until the day is over.

CHAPTER NINE

THE COMPANY 5 firehouse is bigger than the one in Elliott Bay, but everything else is achingly familiar. I'm sure that if I just close my eyes and open them again, Dad will be standing before me in his yellow turnout pants and red suspenders, whistling while he checks over his tools. I even try it . . . just in case. It doesn't make Dad appear, but it does help clear my head.

I breathe in the chemical smell of the foam solution as I follow Uncle Gus across the smooth cement of the apparatus bay. He introduces me to their dispatcher, Kat, and the four guys on shift, including Chet, who looks young enough to be in high school, and Hernando, the one who first found Coco out on the street. His dark eyes dance when he sees her, and he scoops her up with a giant hand and puts his other arm around me. "So good to see

my little *amiga* again. And so good to meet you, Rylee."
He lays his head against Coco's and she licks his bushy
black moustache.

Uncle Gus gives Hernando a fake scowl. "Yeah, thanks
to you buddy, we now have a dog at my house."

Hernando chuckles and winks at me. "Your uncle
should be thanking me, no?"

I bob my head and giggle. "Yep. Coco's awesome."

"Coco, huh? I like it."

He sets her down and grins at me. "Are you hungry,
Rylee? Come try my famous chili relleno."

I throw Uncle Gus a nervous glance. "Chili
what?" I mouth.

"Stuffed chili peppers," he says. "Kinda spicy but
real good."

Hernando leads me to the kitchen and presents a plate
of wizened peppers swimming in a red, cheesy sauce. "How
spicy are they?" I ask.

"Oh, not much," he says, dismissing my worries with a
wave. "Some of my amigos here, they squeal like little girls
if it's too hot. No offense," he adds. He scoops a generous
bite onto a spoon and holds it out.

I gingerly open my mouth, hoping my head doesn't
burst into flames in front of an audience. All I taste at first
is smoky cheese, then a delicious heat follows a few seconds
later, all mixed with crispy batter and juicy pork. "Mmmm,"
I moan, glancing up at the ceiling. "This is awesome."

Hernando pumps his fist like he's won first place in the cooking Olympics. "Yes! You want more?" he asks. "Any time you come here I promise to feed you."

Uncle Gus laughs. "Maybe later," he says, steering me away. "Right now I'm gonna put her to work." He leads the way back out to the bay and slides open a metal cargo drawer on one of the trucks. He reaches beyond the roof cutters and hydraulic tools and grabs a length of soft rope. "Here, this ought to work for your dog. I'll round up a bucket and hose."

"Can I give Coco a tour while you're getting the stuff together?" I ask.

He raises an eyebrow. "A tour? You think she needs one?"

I try to look smug. "If she's going to learn something useful to a fireman, she needs to be familiar with the surroundings."

"Ah," he says, coiling the rope with a thoughtful expression. Coco's busy sniffing one of the truck tires, but I give her leash a quick tug before Uncle Gus can ask more questions. "Be back in a few minutes."

"Okay," he says. "I'll set the stuff out by the ladder truck."

I let Coco meander across the bay before leading her through the kitchen, dormitory and weight room. She takes her time sniffing around the stair stepper and exercise bikes, and I laugh when she jumps on a treadmill. "What," I say, "wanna go for a run?"

I peek inside the empty resource room with its blue plastic chairs and desks and take a minute to picture Dad at the front of the room using the big whiteboard to teach a class. He's not in his wheelchair, though. He stands behind the wooden podium, talking into the mic, wearing the dark blue Cayuse County fire department shirt all the other firemen wear. And faithful Coco snoozes at his feet, waiting patiently until she's needed.

Coco tugs at the leash, pulling me from my daydream, and the image of Dad fades. "Okay," I say. "Let's go."

I let her explore the bay a few minutes longer, weaving through the rows of turnout gear, masks and helmets. If she's going to be a fire education assistant, she has to get used to all the sights and smells and sounds. Once we get home this evening, the official training can begin. I tie her up in the shade near the ladder truck and kiss the top of her head. "Stay here, girl. You can watch me, okay?"

Chet works a few yards away, tightening a bolt on the door hinge of the pumper truck. "I'm impressed," he says, after I've sprayed off the ladder truck and plunged the long handled sponge into the bucket. "I thought you'd ask how to put up the extension pole."

"Naw, I'm a real expert," I say, smiling. "I washed trucks for my dad's company in Elliot Bay."

"You know, I sure was sorry to hear about your dad's accident. How's he doing?"

I pause for a heartbeat, because the question is so much simpler than the answer. How is he compared to before the accident? Pretty awful. But compared to right after the accident? He's terrific. "He's good," I say, because the middle ground seems like the right mix of honest and safe.

"Great," Chet says. "How's school going?"

I use my thumbnail to scrub a splattered bug from the giant headlight. "It's school."

"Yeah, I hear ya'. You gonna join any sports or clubs or anything?"

"Maybe." I swish my bare toes through a puddle of sudsy water and think about the Wednesday Warriors, which makes me think of Miguel and how I wish I'd been nicer to him. "I used to be in a writing group back home."

"No kidding?" Chet says. "I took a semester of creative writing in tenth grade. Wasn't much good, though. Or so the teacher told me."

"What? No! The teacher actually said that?"

He grins. "You know what they say, the truth hurts. But then when I was a junior, I tried my hand at . . ."

The rest of his sentence is drowned out by the deafening tones of the fire alarm. My heart almost shoots straight through the top of my head. But then Chet tosses his wrench into a toolbox and motions for me to pull the hose out of the way, which snaps me out of my stupor.

I quickly drag the hose toward Coco, who is cowering with her tail between her legs. I rush over and scoop her up. "It's okay, girl. It's super loud, huh?"

Uncle Gus studies his pager as he hurries toward the row of gear. He steps into his boots and pulls up his bunker pants in one smooth move before motioning me over. "Come on, Rylee. Better come along with me."

Goose bumps race up my spine and explode across my scalp. "Really?" I mouth.

He shrugs on his heavy Kevlar coat. "Structure fire," he says. Then he grins. "And I don't trust you here alone with the chili relleno." Before I can say anything more he takes Coco from my arms and holds her out to Kat the dispatcher. "Mind dog-sitting?"

She extends willing arms and makes a kissy face at Coco. "Oooh, not at all."

The thought of leaving Coco with a stranger makes my heart flip. But Kat flashes a reassuring smile. "Don't worry, Rylee. I've got some puppy treats right here in my desk. She'll be fine." And I decide to trust her because there's no time left and too much noise to think.

Uncle Gus waves his gloves in front of my face. "Come on, girl. Let's roll. Jump seat of the pumper."

I scramble up the steps into the truck and nearly lose my flip-flops in the process. Hernando pushes a button before climbing in next to me as the huge metal station door clatters up its track. I fumble with my seat belt and yank it tight as Uncle Gus hops into the driver's seat with Chet beside him. The big engine vibrates to life, and I brace my feet as we roll out onto Independence Avenue with the EMS van leading the way.

Hernando cocks an eyebrow at me. "The firefighters I work with, they get younger all the time."

I laugh. "I know. I can't believe Uncle Gus is letting me go."

He chuckles, and white teeth flash beneath his moustache. "Firefighting runs in your family, no?"

We speed through the outskirts of Cayuse, past alfalfa fields and fruit orchards, the siren at full wail. I haven't been on a ride along in six months, and I turn my face to the window so Hernando doesn't catch me grinning like an idiot. I can't help it. There's something unbelievably cool about a fire truck—the powerful rumble shaking my seat, the commanding siren that makes people stop and gawk, how it parts traffic as slick as God parting the Red Sea. I think about what Hernando said, about firefighting running in my family, and it makes me ache for Dad in a whole new way. He loves everything about firefighting. He used to talk about it so much that sometimes Mom would roll her eyes and say, "Honestly, Mike, get a life."

Dad just *has* to be a fireman—for himself and for me.

Hernando interrupts me with a shoulder bump. He points to a field with plants of papery green clusters trailing up tall guide wires. "Know what those are?"

"Hops," I say, proudly.

He gives me a thumbs up. "*Si*" he says, "can't have beer without 'em."

Five minutes later we turn off the main road into a subdivision of nice homes, with sleek cars parked in the driveways and yards overflowing with flowers. The neighborhood feels vaguely familiar, but I don't know why until I spot the bunch of brightly painted iron poppies Mom fell in love with when we first moved here, and I realize we're only a few blocks from Uncle Gus's house.

Halfway down the street smoke blocks the sun. The truck slows and eases up before a garage swallowed with flames. Smoke billows up thick and acrid, and tiny bits of soot and debris swirl like a dirty blizzard. Several yards away a boy kneels on the lawn with his hands over his face. He's bent over something furry and white, and my heart instantly lands in my throat. "Oh, no," I breath. "What is that, Uncle Gus?"

"Cat or dog," he says, turning over his shoulder. "Chet?"

"I'm on it," Chet says, hopping down the steps as soon as the truck rolls to a stop. I stay out of the way while Hernando hustles past and then scramble up front to watch through the huge windshield. Uncle Gus and the others fan out toward the flaming garage, but Chet grabs the pet revival equipment and hurries to join the medic who's already reached the boy.

The boy's still crouched over the little animal, his shoulders shaking, and watching is almost more than I can bear. It forces me back to those first horrible, gut wrenching hours Mom and I spent in the hospital, desperate for news about Dad, yet terrified what we might hear.

I know I'm not allowed to get out of the truck, but right then I don't care. I jump down the steps and jog over to the small group on the lawn. A few feet away, I recognize the slope of the boy's shoulders and the way his black hair curls around his ears. But even with the few seconds of warning, I'm still caught off guard when he raises his head and I catch my first glimpse of his face.

Miguel!

CHAPTER TEN

T HE ANIMAL LYING limp in front of Miguel is a big tabby, with silky white fur and four tan paws. Miguel has a hand wrapped around one of the cat's hind legs, like he can't bear to let go, and there's so much grief rolling off him it rocks me back on my heels.

For a few seconds, I'm too frozen by the weird coincidence to know how to act. I was such a jerk the last time we talked, I'm probably the last person Miguel wants to see. But hiding from him at a time like this would make me an even bigger jerk, and I just can't make myself do it. I step into view. "Hey, Miguel."

He turns my way, dazed, and then he blinks. "Oh ... wow, Rylee?"

"Yeah. Are you okay?"

He shrugs and then ducks away, and I know he's struggling not to cry in front of me.

I creep forward and drop down on my knees beside Chet. "Is this your cat, Miguel?"

"My brother's," he says, his voice cracking. He takes off his glasses and rubs his eyes. "He loves to sleep in the garage. I went for him first thing … but I was too late."

He's broken a serious rule I've had drummed into my head since I was little. You never go into a burning building to rescue an animal—not unless you're a trained first responder anyway. I glance at Chet to gauge his reaction, but he's unwrapping the coiled tubing attached to the oxygen bottle and doesn't respond. The medic doesn't scold Miguel either. She just keeps patting his back. "It might not be too late," she says. "It may only be smoke inhalation."

Chet runs gentle hands over the cat, probing for a heartbeat, assessing any injuries. "What's this handsome guy's name?" he asks.

"T-Thomas," Miguel says. "Is he … I mean, is there any way you can save him?"

I have no idea how much experience Chet has resuscitating animals, but he offers Miguel a confident smile and settles Thomas across his lap. "I'm sure gonna give it my very best shot," he says. "Let's see what we can do here." He gently lifts the cat's limp head, fits a small plastic mask over Thomas' face and attaches it with a rubber strap behind his ears. "Okay now Thomas," he croons. "Come on back to us, buddy. No victims today. Come on, Thomas."

Miguel watches, breathless, his face screwed tight with a mix of despair and hope. I can barely breathe myself as a powerful pressure builds inside my chest, growing bigger and bigger until everything else around us seems to shrink. It's like a huge bubble has formed around the four of us and Thomas. Nothing else exists—no fire, or smoke or noise.

The medic keeps thumping Miguel's back, and Chet keeps stroking and murmuring to Thomas. I don't know how much time passes, maybe two minutes, maybe five, but I can tell Miguel is giving up as he crumples closer and closer to the lawn. All I can think about is how devastated I'd be if it was Coco, and my heart breaks for him.

A sudden blaze of silver flashes my face and I squint over to see an SUV race into the driveway, spitting gravel as it jerks to a stop. "My dad," Miguel says, keeping his eyes on Thomas. A slender man in black jeans and a polo jumps out of the car, his face a panicked question mark. Then he spots Miguel and rushes over. "Son?"

Miguel wipes his face. "I'm okay, Dad. But... Thomas..."

His dad regards the cat with a pained expression before turning away with a grim nod. The medic introduces herself and Chet, and then scoots aside so Miguel's dad can have her place. He crouches down beside Miguel. "What happened, son?"

Miguel shoves his glasses back on. "I was in my room, and all of a sudden I smelled smoke and all I could think about was getting Thomas out. But I don't know how the fire started."

His dad is silent for a moment, then his eyes flare and he puts a fist to his mouth. "Oh, my God," he says. "Maybe it was me. I don't remember turning off the coffee pot this morning."

I briefly wonder why anyone would keep a coffee pot in their garage, but then the thought flees my brain as Thomas' rib cage stutters with a shallow flutter. "Hey!" Miguel cries, pointing. "He moved ... he moved." No one answers him. We're all too focused on Thomas.

I'm afraid to blink, not sure if I actually saw something or not. And I'm thinking how awful for Miguel to think he's alive when he's really dead after all. But then Thomas takes another breath ... and one more.

Yes!" Chet says, grinning. "That's what we're after."

Miguel clutches his face with a sob of joy, and I cover my mouth and squeeze my eyes hard, because it's darn tough not to cry when you've just witnessed a miracle. The medic wipes her eyes and then reaches over and gives Miguel a high five. "Congratulations," she says. "You got your kitty back."

Miguel's dad is staring blankly, like he's still frozen by the idea he may have caused the fire. But then Miguel grabs his arm and starts jerking. "Dad! Look at Thomas, Dad," and he snaps out of his fog and hugs Miguel. "I see," he says. "I see."

Chet keeps the mask in place as Thomas lifts his head and tries to gaze around, but when Thomas tries to shake his head, Chet removes it. "How's that feel? Huh, buddy? Welcome back."

"You saved him," Miguel's dad says. "I can't believe it."

"Sometimes a little oxygen works wonders," Chet says, smiling. Then he lifts the cat and hands him to Miguel. "Here you go. He's gonna be fine."

Miguel's hands tremble as he takes Thomas and cradles him against his chest. "Thank you. Thank you so much."

Hernando comes over to talk with Miguel's dad then, and Chet joins them as they step toward the house. "Why don't you kids take Thomas and sit in the shade for a while," the medic suggests. "Make sure he doesn't go near the fire."

"Okay," Miguel says, as he climbs to his feet. He looks at me and smiles.

"Come on," I say, smiling back. "We can go sit in the truck."

"The truck?" he echoes, looking around like he can't possibly figure out what I'm talking about.

I giggle and point to the fire truck. "Yeah, see that big red truck with the flashing light bar? You can't miss it."

Miguel's eyes widen. "Are you sure we're supposed to?"

"Yeah, it's fine," I say, leading the way. I scramble up into the truck and over to the driver's seat. Miguel climbs up behind me, still looking like he expects to get yelled at any second. He slowly settles into the passenger seat, careful not to jostle Thomas who's peering around with narrowed yellow eyes. It occurs to me he's probably thirsty, so I grab a water bottle off the floor and fill a Thermos cup half full. "Here you go, Thomas. Need a drink?"

Thomas sniffs at the water for a few seconds before his raspy tongue shoots out and starts delicately lapping. "Yay," I say, smiling. "Guess so." I hand the rest of the bottle to Miguel. "Here, you should have some too."

"Thanks." Miguel drains the rest of the bottle and then goes back to watching Thomas, his eyes still full of wonder. "Man," he says, with a shaky laugh, "the day started out so normal."

I sniff. "Yeah, weird how fast things can go south, huh? So, your dad keeps a coffee maker in the garage?"

Miguel nods. "Yeah, it's his office. He likes to drink coffee and listen to music when he writes."

"Oh. And he thinks he might have forgotten to turn it off?"

"Wouldn't be the first time." He glances at me. "Could that really start a fire?"

"Maybe," I say. "If the pot was empty and the burner stayed hot. My uncle might be able to tell."

"Your uncle?"

I point to one of the figures shrouded in the smoke. "Yeah, that's him over there. The guy with the red hat. He's a captain."

"Oh." His gaze sweeps across all the dials and switches and gauges in front of him. "So that's why it's okay for us to sit in here. Sweet truck."

A zing of pride zips though me. "I know, right?" But then we both get quiet, and things start to feel awkward. I wipe my palms on my thighs and struggle to think of something more to say. "So, Thomas is your brother's cat?"

Miguel scratches behind the cat's ears. "Yeah. He got all A's on his report card in fourth grade, so Thomas was his reward."

"Nice. He doesn't know about the fire yet, does he?"

"Uh … no. He's not home right now."

The way he says it makes me curious, but something tells me not to snoop. We both look out at the garage, which is turning into a soaked, blackened shell. Columns of white smoke rise where the powerful jet of the hose douses the burning wood. "I still can't believe this whole thing," Miguel says.

"Did you guys have anything important in there? Besides Thomas?" I quickly add.

Miguel considers this. "Dad always keeps his laptop with him, so his writing stuff should be okay. But there was his desk and an old couch and … " He winces. "Oh, jeez, my longboard. My longboard's in there. I've only had it a few months."

"Your parents must have insurance," I say. "I bet they'll pay for a new one."

He brightens. "I hope so," he says, before his expression turns questioning. "So...do you usually go to fires?"

"Oh, no. I was down at the station washing trucks when the call came in and my uncle let me come."

"Is this the first one you've ever been to?"

"Nope. My dad used to let me go once in a while when we lived in Oregon. Not to medical calls, but sometimes if it was just a one alarm fire or something."

"One alarm? Does that mean it's not too serious?"

"Not exactly," I say. "It has more to do with the first dispatch, when the call comes in and they decide how many trucks and firefighters they need. If they send the right amount the first time, then it's a one alarm. But if it turns out to be bigger than they thought, or they need more help for some other reason it turns into a two or even three alarm fire."

Miguel looks impressed I have this kind of knowledge, and it makes my heart swell. "Cool," he says. "So your dad's a fireman too?"

My fingers tighten around the corded edge of the seat as the good feeling evaporates. "Yeah, he is. Just not right now. He got in a bad car accident."

His eyes narrow and I can see his brain turning over the information. "When?"

"A few months ago. When we lived in Oregon. That's why we moved here, so my uncle could help us for a while."

"Oh. He must've got hurt pretty bad for you to have to move."

I let out a soft breath. "Yeah...he did." I turn away and glance out the window at Miguel's dad. He's standing alone now, gazing at the scene with droopy shoulders, still looking kind of stunned, like he can't believe he might've played a role in something so awful.

I know exactly how he feels—I've been feeling it for three months.

"I think he's starting to feel better," Miguel says, and for a moment I'm confused. But then I see Thomas rubbing against his hand, and I realize he means the cat.

"That's great," I say. "Your dad doesn't look too happy, though."

Miguel lets out a big breath. "I'm just glad I'm not the one in trouble."

And I can't help but smile, because even though it's not very sympathetic, I totally get what he means. "So," I say, "your dad likes music when he writes?"

"Yep. Says it helps him concentrate. Makes him more creative."

"I'm kind of like that too," I say. "I can't think if it's super quiet. How about you? Do you like quiet or noise when you write?"

He hesitates for a few seconds. "Actually," he says, "I like quiet. That's why I have a clandestine writing spot."

My smirk slips out before I can stop it. "Clandestine? Wow, can you even spell that?"

"Yep," he says, smiling. "C-l-a-n-d-e-s-t-i-n-e. It's a way cooler word than secret, don't you think?"

"I guess," I admit. "And where is this clandestine spot of yours?"

"At the Chateau St. Michelle Winery."

"Don't you have to be twenty-one to go in those places?"

His face scrunches like I said something ridiculous and my ears burn. "I don't go for the wine tasting," he says with a laugh. "I stay in an area out back where nobody ever goes, and my mom can't find me to make me do chores."

"Oh. How far is it?"

"Not far." He pauses for a minute. "I'll show you some-time . . . if you want."

Sweat pops out on my palms. I'm relieved he's not mad at me for our last conversation, and I'm super glad I got to be here for Thomas' rescue. But now it feels like I might be walking into a trap. Hanging around outside of school is not what kinda friends do, it's what real friends do. And we are not real friends. But I don't want to come off as a jerk again either. "Maybe," I say.

Miguel's dad is gazing aimlessly around, his phone pressed to his ear.

"I better go," Miguel says. "He's probably wondering where I am."

"Oh yeah, sure," I say. "I'm really glad Thomas is okay."

Miguel gives me a grateful smile. "Thanks. Me too."

He scrambles down to the ground, then pauses to glance back. "See you at school Monday?"

And I nod, "Okay."

By the time I get home later it's three o'clock, and I'm impatient to start working with Coco. But first I just have to tell Dad about the fire. He listens eagerly, and his eyes light up when I describe what it was like to see Thomas take his first breath. "It was just like when you saved Mrs. Ripley's poodle," I say. "It was amazing."

"It feels great when things work out," he says. "I'm glad for Chet."

"For Chet?"

"Yeah," Dad says. "Losing any victim rips you apart, two legged or four. You take it personal, even if you did all you could. But when there's a happy ending … man, you feel like a hero." He gazes off above my head then, and I can tell from his smile he's recalling some of his own happy endings, the times he was a hero. And it opens up a deep longing inside me, because I want so bad to give him that feeling back, to make him happy again. All I have to do is make Coco into the best fire education partner the world's ever seen. She will be the bridge to get both of us back to the place we need to be.

Dad turns his focus back to me and winks. "I'm glad Gus took you along, but your mom might not be too thrilled."

"You used to take me sometimes."

"Yeah, but that was me. And you always stayed in the truck."

"Then don't tell her," I say, lowering my voice even though Mom's not in the room. "It can be our little secret, just like the dandelions."

Dad's brows knit. "Dandelions?"

"Well...yeah," I say, devastated he could forget something so important. "I used to cry when Mom made you mow them, remember? Until you told me they had special powers that made them come back even bigger and stronger."

"Ahh," he says, smiling. "Now I remember. The hidden powers of a dandelion." He nods. "Okay then, our secret."

"Our secret," I repeat softly as I back away. "Don't forget."

I turn to find Coco gone. But after a quick search I discover her sprawled in my bedroom, a tiny heap of colorful material between her feet. She raises her ears and bares her teeth in a smile.

"What is that, girl? Whatcha' got?" I stoop for a closer look and my breath hitches. It's a pair of Mom's underwear—satiny blue with green polka dots—completely shredded. My whole body tingles. "No, stop!" I hiss. "Bad girl. Bad Coco."

Her tail goes still and her ears droop. I feel terrible, but I keep the glare on my face anyway. Mom's just tolerating a dog as it is. The last thing she needs is more reason not to like her. "Bad," I say again, wondering when she found time to steal a pair of underwear in the few minutes we've been home.

"Hey, Rylee," Mom calls, and my heart triples its speed. "Now that you're home I could use your help for a bit."

"Oh…sure," I say. "Coming." I wad the underwear and shove them under my air mattress. Maybe she'll assume the dryer ate them. Better yet, maybe she'll never miss them at all.

Mom puts me to work flattening cardboard boxes as she empties them. She asks about my day, and I tell her about meeting the fire station crew, and about getting to try the great chili relleno. Part of me wishes I could tell her about the fire and Thomas, but I know Dad's right. Mom's more protective of me since the accident, she probably wouldn't like that Uncle Gus took me along. Besides, it's nice to share something special with Dad. It reminds me of the way things used to be when we shared lots of stuff, just the two of us.

As soon as I finish helping Mom, I snap on Coco's leash and escape to the back yard. I offer her one of the feta cheese crumbles I snuck from the fridge, and she sucks it down like a vacuum cleaner, her eyes eager for more. "No more freebies," I say, shaking my finger at her. "You have to earn the rest." I'm not sure how to go about teaching a dog to stop, drop and roll, but it makes sense to go in order.

I walk in a slow circle around the yard, holding Coco close to my leg. Every few yards I say, "Stop," and pull her up short, letting a cheese crumble drop in front of her nose. Whenever she tries to pull away or gets distracted, I crinkle the plastic treat bag to get her attention. Then I move forward and do it again. The ten cheese crumbles are gone in only a few minutes, but it's not a problem. I've watched enough YouTube videos to know dogs learn best in short bursts of training.

I drop down on the grass and Coco flops across my lap. "You did awesome," I say, rubbing her belly. "Absolutely awesome." I find just the right spot to scratch so that she starts to kick her hind leg. "You funny girl," I say, giggling. Then I pull the stuffed octopus from my other pocket and wave it in front her. "Want to pull another leg off, huh? You made it a quatrapus. Soon it will be a unipus."

She attacks with ferocious growls, bracing all four legs and jerking like she's trying to yank her teeth out. She's surprisingly strong for her size and I wonder how big she'll get. Beagles are about thirty pounds full grown, but I'm convinced she's a puggle. At least I'm going to say she is, just so I can keep uttering that awesome word. Not that her breed matters anyway. What kid could resist her? Every school around will request a visit. Dad will be so busy teaching and educating, he won't have time to miss the parts of firefighting he can't do anymore. Shoot, he'll be so popular the other guys will be drooling with envy.

"What other useful stuff should you know?" I ask out loud, but Coco's too bent on destroying her octopus to pay any attention. Teaching her to crawl would make sense, like she's trying to escape a smoky room. Or how to play dead. And maybe I *will* train her how to climb a ladder, just to prove Dad wrong.

"Rylee?" Mom appears at my side.

"Oh, hey," I say, glancing up with a smile. But Mom's serious expression stops me cold. All I can think of is the shredded underwear, how she must have discovered them already. But then I realize that no, this is more serious, and my heart stutters. I release the octopus and Coco tumbles backwards. "What's the matter? Is it Dad?"

She shakes her head. "Dad's fine. I just . . ." She spreads her hands in a helpless gesture that scares me silly. "I have to tell you something you're not gonna want to hear."

I clench my teeth, and it sends a white hot jolt through my jaw. If it's not Dad, what then? "Is Uncle Gus . . . ?"

"He's fine too."

I scramble to my feet. "What then?" I demand, fighting the impulse to cover my ears.

"Gus just called, honey. They found Coco's owner."

Four words. They probably took only a couple of seconds to spill out, but it seems more like half an hour. I stare at Mom. "No they didn't," I say.

Mom winces. "It's some guy who claims his wife was running errands when Coco got out of the car. He says they've been searching everywhere." She places both hands on her neck. "Gus is bringing him here to see her."

The world goes foggy, and I stumble back clutching my head. "No! No he can't."

"Sweetie, I know you've gotten attached to her. I'm sorry." She reaches for me.

My chest fills with sharp, agonizing pain, and I'm not sure if I'm having a panic attack or a heart attack. "He can't have her, Mom. Don't let them take her. Please. . . She's mine!" I scoop Coco up and stumble for the house.

"Rylee, honey?" Mom calls, sounding alarmed. "It'll be okay. Maybe once Dad's better we can get you another dog."

There's no point in answering. She doesn't get it. I make it to my room and sprawl across the air mattress. Everything swims around me, distorted in size and shape, and I'm sweating buckets. I close my eyes, but the motion keeps going anyway. Then I realize it's me moving, rocking Coco back and forth as the muscles jump beneath my hot skin.

There has to be some mistake. After all we've been through, after everything I've already lost. I can't lose Coco. How can I save Dad without her? How can I save myself? I drop my face to hers and she licks frantically at my tears.

I don't know how much time passes, maybe ten minutes, maybe thirty. But I'm still lost in a thick fog when Mom taps at my door. "Honey, your uncle's here."

I don't answer. I can't.

Mom steps into my room. "Rylee," she says, her voice kind but firm. "I know this is really tough for you, but what if it was your dog and you'd been searching for her?"

I hate her right then. I hate her for being right. "You're probably glad," I say. "You never wanted her anyway."

Mom blinks, then looks away for a moment before she sighs. "You're right," she says. "I didn't. But I do like that she's your friend. Do you want me to take her out?"

My eyes fill with fresh tears and I brush them away. "No." I push myself to my feet and creep out to the porch. Uncle Gus is standing in the yard beside a skinny guy with a goatee and ripped jeans. A sour taste rises to my mouth.

Uncle Gus glances at me, his eyes full of apology. He clears his throat. "Rylee, this is Mr. Carson."

The man whirls toward me, his lips parting in a lopsided grin when he sees Coco. "Well, well ... there's the little rascal. Been scouring the whole county for you."

I gaze past the man to his beat-up red pickup. A Rottweiler hangs out the passenger window, his tongue lolling drops of saliva—the kind of monster that could gulp Coco down in two bites. I think I might throw up.

"We live on out by the fairgrounds," the man continues. "That's why it took till now to see the poster at the fire station."

Mom hovers protectively beside me, like she expects my knees to buckle at any moment. She deserves credit for pretending to care, even if she really doesn't. "How exactly did you lose your dog?" she asks.

"The missus was shopping at Super One when the rascal squeezed right through the window and took off. Sure did. Left the window down a bit too much, I guess. She's gonna be so happy. Thought the little beggar was gone for good."

"I see," Mom says. "And ... and you're sure this is your dog?"

"Oh, yeah. That's Little Jack, all right."

A rushing fills my ears and my head shoots up. "W-what?" I stammer. "What did you just say?"

The man looks confused. "I said, that's him. The missus calls him Little Jack."

My heart surges and I struggle for a breath. "Coco's not a boy. She's a girl!"

Mom puts her fingertips over her mouth.

The man scratches his goatee. "What? Now wait a cotton pickin' minute." He fumbles for his phone. "It's him. Got a picture right here to prove it."

I throw Uncle Gus a desperate look. "She's not his dog, Uncle Gus. She can't be." I turn Coco to face him, belly out. "See?"

A smile plays on his lips. "Well, look there, Mr. Carson. I guess that isn't your pup after all."

Mr. Carson scrolls through his photos for several more seconds before glancing up with a huff. "I was sure I had a picture. Just can't find it right now."

Uncle Gus scratches the back of his head. "Well, picture or no, if you lost a male, this can't be your dog."

Mr. Carson screws up his face like he's about to spit and sputter, but no sound comes out. Or maybe it does, but I can't hear it over my own crazy laugh. I'm suddenly energized enough to do a dozen cartwheels in a row. "Sorry you wasted your time," I say, as graciously as I can. "Hope you find Little Jack soon." Then I twirl around and scurry inside with Coco clutched tight.

I hover inside the door, my chest heaving, until the old pickup finally rattles out of the drive. Then I peek around with a shaky grin. "Is it safe to come out now?"

Mom puts her hands on her hips. "Oh good grief," she says. "I did not like that guy."

I set Coco down on the lawn as Uncle Gus comes over and wraps his arms around me. "Sorry kiddo. He showed up out of the blue."

I hug him back, blinking away happy tears. "It's okay," I say, not bothering to add I would forgive him anything in the world right then.

"Do you think he even lost a dog?" Mom asks. "He seemed pretty sketchy."

"Not sure," Uncle Gus says. "But my gut tells me you're right."

I step back from Uncle Gus. "Do me a favor?" I ask. "Take down that stupid poster at the fire station and throw it away, or burn it, or shred it ... or destroy it however you want."

He chuckles. "Tell me how you really feel."

Mom smiles. "Wow, okay then." She heads for the porch. "Now that the latest disaster has been averted, I'm going inside to make spaghetti."

I like how Mom refers to it as a disaster, and I'm sorry for my mean comment earlier. I hope she knows I didn't mean it.

"And I'm headed to the shower," Uncle Gus says, "and then to see if that brother of mine is up for watching some football." He pulls his wallet from his back pocket and hands me ten dollars. "For truck washing services rendered."

"Oh, thanks," I say, taking the money. "You don't have to pay me though, you know? It was fun."

"What was? Washing trucks, or talking to that cute boy at the fire?"

Heat blazes up my neck and fans my face. "Miguel? He's just some kid I know from school."

"Oh, yeah? That why you invited him to sit in the truck?"

I do my best to squelch a horrified giggle but it comes out anyway. "What? No! He needed a place to sit with Thomas. Jeez, I was only trying to be nice."

Uncle Gus winks. "Whatever you say, Rylee. No need to get all worked up."

I stamp my foot and turn my back on him as he walks away laughing. I picture Miguel's crazy eyebrows and the way his mop of dark hair falls over his forehead. So, yeah, he is pretty cute. Not that I need my family's opinion.

Coco has discovered her octopus again and is playing tug of war by herself, pinning the body between her stubby paws while jerking on another leg. She's so cute and incredible, and I can't believe I just came within an inch of losing her. It's an impossible thought, almost too big to think about, and it makes my knees go weak.

I pick a nearby dandelion and sit cross legged beside Coco. I twirl the flower against my chin until I'm sure there's a yellow mark. Then I gently spin the flower on Coco's smooth belly to create a faint circle. "That's it," I tell her. "We have both been bestowed with the super powers of a dandelion. Feel any different?"

She offers me a goofy look and thumps her tail. "Doesn't matter," I say, giggling. "You are destined to do great things. Even greater than ripping off the legs of an octopus."

My phone vibrates. "Hold that thought," I tell Coco, shading the screen against the sun's glare. *Kara Bryant.* The name gives me a happy twinge. She's a Wednesday Warrior, and except for an occasional comment on Instagram, we haven't talked since leaving Elliott Bay. I swipe my thumb to answer. "Hey, Kara. Hi."

There's a sudden sharp breath followed by silence. "Hello?" I say. "It's Rylee. Is this Kara?"

"No," says a flutter soft voice. "Kara let me borrow her phone."

Goosebumps explode up my arms. For three months I've done my best to avoid her, to block her. But she's finally outsmarted me. "What do you want, Molly?"

"Just to talk, Rylee. Please don't hang up." Her words are shaky and uncertain, not at all the full, confident voice I know so well.

"To talk?" I echo in disbelief. "Seriously? I begged you to talk right after the police showed us the picture, and you wouldn't say anything."

"Only because I couldn't. I told you--"

"Doesn't matter," I interrupt. "I already know what happened anyway."

Another shaky breath. "No you don't. You don't know the whole story."

"It was you and Carla," I say. "What else is there to know?"

"Yes, we were there," Molly says, her voice choked with tears. "But if you'd seen the whole video you'd understand."

My pulse is slamming my neck, and my thumb trembles over the *end call* symbol. I want so badly to hang up. I'm not sure what's stopping me. "You should see my dad, Molly. You should see what it's like for him now."

"I'm so sorry, Rylee," she says, in a desperate rush. "But I can't stand you thinking it was all my fault."

I swallow. *I know it wasn't*, I want to say, *it was mine too.* But it's nearly impossible to think those words, much less say them out loud. "Talking won't fix what happened," I say. "So quit trying. I'm hanging up now."

"No, Rylee, wait,' she pleads. "Over hills and mounds … remember?"

I close my eyes as my insides crumble. Things between us weren't supposed to end … not ever. And certainly not the way they did. No friendship should ever end that way. But I just can't go there. And it's too late now anyway. I hang up, and drop the phone on the lawn like it's something dangerous.

Coco's watching me, focused as only a dog can be. She crawls over and starts to lick my hand like she knows something is wrong. And I stretch out on the grass next to her, because the sound of Molly's voice has rattled all my bones so loose they can no longer support me.

CHAPTER ELEVEN

W E ARE IN *fourth grade the first time Mom allows us to ride to the highway overpass near my house. We stow our scooters in the tumbleweeds at the base of the massive steel girders and I prance up the winding metal staircase. We have played at each other's homes and at school, but this is the very first time I have taken the lead in deciding what to do, the first time I've gotten to take you to a place you've never been. I feel so proud of myself, so confident and incredibly grown up. We breathe in the smell of diesel in the cool afternoon breeze and squeal at the swaying sensation as the traffic rushes below. We skip halfway across the span of cement and sit on the single wooden bench.*

"Here's what I got," I say, emptying my pockets. "What did you bring?"

We set out lipstick in mauve madness and pink passion, blush and eye shadow in various shades of blue and green and gray. Makeup we have stolen from our mothers. Makeup we are not yet allowed to wear. We discuss face shape and skin tone as if we're experts. We purse our lips and make fish faces into your little round mirror. We place beaded Bobbie pins in our hair in various ways to make ourselves look as sophisticated as the high school girls. We are both wearing half zipped sweatshirts and black leggings and look a little like twins.

"Wouldn't it be cool if we were sisters?" you say, and I nod, without admitting I wish that very thing all the time.

"Let's make a special pledge," I say, "to promise we'll be best friends forever."

"You don't have to promise that sort of thing," you say. "You just do it."

But you make friends much more easily than me, and I don't think you realize you are my only good friend, the only friend I have ever spent the night with. I'm not sure how to explain my fear that without some kind of promise, you'll make an even better friend and leave me behind. I don't know how to explain my desperate need to keep you all to myself. So I force a smile, like it's not nearly as important as it is. "Just for the fun of it," I say.

"Like those friendship necklaces Shayla and Maddie have?" you ask. "The ones that each have half a heart?"

I shrug. "Yeah, or maybe just a poem or something."

You stare into the mirror and dab on mauve lipstick. "I'm no good at poetry. You come up with something."

"Okay," I say, and I think hard and long. Then I have it, and I make you lock pinkies with me as I teach you our new secret pledge.

Through ups and downs
Over hills and mounds
Despite fads or trends
We will always be best friends

CHAPTER TWELVE

I SWEEP MOLLY FROM my mind like dirt into a corner and focus all my attention on training Coco. Whenever Mom takes a nap or a shower, or gets on the phone with some insurance person, I steal out to the backyard with Coco. I don't think I'm superstitious—not in the black-cat, step-on-a-crack kind of way—but I can't shake the worry that if anyone catches wind of my plan before I'm ready, they'll laugh. And when people laugh at me, I doubt myself, and it might end up jinxing the whole thing.

But if I can just keep a grip on Coco's big reveal until the perfect time, I know everybody will be jaw dropping impressed—especially Dad. Because Coco is an amazing student, smart and eager to please. I discover that she loves cheese crumbles and apples, goes gaga over Ritz-Bitz, and is offended by sweet pickles. I trade the pickles for peanuts, and by the time the jar is a third gone, Coco has mastered stop, drop, and roll. I want to teach her to crawl next. And I've watched enough YouTube to know how, but I need a bigger, more private place.

The Friday before Columbus Day, as Mr. Hinkle drones on about our homework assignment for the three day weekend, I finally get an idea. Why not bring Coco right back here to school to work with her? There's no soccer games scheduled, so the field should be empty, and if we stay behind the building nobody can see us. It's perfect!

I'm so busy feeling smart, I don't notice Miguel as he trails me out of science class. I've never actually invited him to walk with me, but I kinda like when he does. He's funny and friendly and offers good writing advice. He makes a great surface friend.

Today, we're walking along like two bobbing shadows, each thinking our own thoughts, when a shriek makes us spin to the left. A little curly haired girl is hugging a tree like her life depends on it. A lady wearing a foot brace, who I assume is her mom, tries to tug her away.

"Is she just throwing a tantrum?" I ask Miguel.

His eyebrows scrunch. "Maybe," he says, "but I don't think so."

Before I can ask what he's basing this on, he heads toward them and I instinctively follow. The lady catches sight of us and grimaces. "It's not as dire as it seems," she says, sounding ashamed. "My daughter's just upset about her kitten."

"What kitten?" Miguel and I ask at the exact same second. He grins at me, and I snort with embarrassment.

The lady relaxes some and points up into the tree. "He went up like a shot, but he can't figure out how to come down."

We move closer to peer into the leafy canopy. It's a massive old weeping willow with a few thick branches leading to a zillion twiggy, arching ones. I can barely make out an orange and white kitten about two thirds of the way up, perched in a little V formed by two slender branches. He's peeking down at us through the leaves, mewing pitifully. "Jeez," I say. "He's pretty high. Too bad we don't have one of the fire truck ladders."

Miguel nods and bumps up his glasses. "No kidding," he says.

The little girl's bottom lip is almost touching the ground, and I feel bad for her. I squat down and meet her eyes. "Is that your kitty up there? What's his name?"

She turns watery eyes up at her mom, like she needs permission to answer a stranger, and I suddenly feel a lot older. "O-oscar," she blubbers.

"Oscar, huh? I like that. And what's your name?"

"Melanie," she says, holding up three fingers. "I'm this many."

"Nice to meet you," I say. "I'm Rylee, and that's Miguel."

The lady smiles. "And I'm Margo," she says. "The bad mom who let Oscar escape."

Miguel is still craning his neck up at Oscar. "How long's he been up there?"

"Fifteen, twenty minutes."

"Has he climbed that high before?"

Margo scrapes a hand over her face. "No, we usually don't let him out of the house. But I opened the door to grab the mail, and right then this loud car zoomed by and he freaked." She gestures to her foot brace. "Not much I can do about it."

Miguel slips off his backpack. "It's okay. I'll get him."

"Oh, no," Margo says. "You don't have to."

"I'll get him," Miguel repeats, determination in his voice.

"No," she insists, sounding equally determined. "You might get hurt, and then what will your parents say?"

He flicks her an impatient glance. "It's not a problem. My brother and I used to climb trees all the time." His words are short and clipped, almost rude, and I'm surprised by this side of him. Then I remember how he ran into the burning garage to save Thomas, and I figure either he really adores cats, or he just wants to be a hero. It reminds me of one of Dad's favorite sayings. *If you jump in to save a drowning person and you both drown, that makes you dead, not a hero.*

"Are you sure you know what you're doing?" I ask Miguel.

It comes out more skeptical than I mean it to, and Miguel frowns. "Thanks for the vote of confidence."

Heat rushes to my cheeks. Before I can think of a reply, Miguel makes a hop for the lowest branch.

Melanie is suddenly too fascinated to cry. She stares wide-eyed at Miguel, her mouth hanging open, like he's got super powers of unimaginable ability. And I wonder if that's how I looked when Dad first told me about the dandelions. I smile at her. "Guess what, Melanie? Oscar's gonna be just fine."

Margo doesn't look convinced. She has her fingertips on her cheek and is shaking her head. "Oh … careful, careful," she begs, as Miguel hoists himself higher. "Please don't get hurt, or it will be my fault." She pulls Melanie back from the tree, as if she expects Miguel to tumble down and squash her.

I lean against the trunk and squint up at Miguel. He's being careful, testing each branch before trusting it with his weight. But the bark is smooth, and his sneakers are nothing special. If he falls, he'll splat right onto the bare, hard packed ground. My palms turn sweaty. "Hey," I call. "Doing okay up there?"

He shoulders through a bunch of twiggy foliage before he answers. "Yeah, I'm good. It's hard to see through all the leaves though. Can you see the kitten?"

I have to back up several steps to spot him. "He's to your right," I call. "You have to go right."

"But he's still above me, isn't he?"

"Yeah. Maybe another ten feet or so."

Melanie's mom is making soft, worried sounds in the back of her throat. "Tell him to come down," she says. "We'll find some other way."

But I'm too busy coaching Miguel to answer her. "Good," I call up to him. "You're doing good."

"How close am I?" he asks a few minutes later.

"Can't tell for sure," I say. "He's still off to your right. Maybe another five feet or so."

"Oh … yeah, I see him now," Miguel says, his breath ragged. "Come 'ere, Oscar. Here kitty, kitty."

"Oh, whoa!" he shouts, and my heart almost stops as a shower of debris and leaves rains down on me.

Margo gasps. "Oh, be careful, be careful! I can't watch."

I spit out a piece of bark. "Hey, are you okay, Miguel?"

Several seconds of silence follow. I think of Dad's accident, how a perfectly normal day can turn tragic in the blink of an eye, and my stomach rolls. "What are you doing?" I demand. "Are you okay, Miguel?"

"Yeah," he finally says, "but I knocked my glasses off."

I'm not sure whether this is good news or bad. "So… can you see anything?"

"Not much," he says. "Oh … wait. Here they are. I've got 'em. I lost track of Oscar again though."

My heart is still thudding as I back up. "You're almost to him," I say. "A couple feet above you and … to your right."

I can't see Miguel's arm, but I do see his fingers as they close around Oscar. "You got him," I yell, bouncing on my toes. "You got him."

"Does he?" Margo asks, breathless. "Does he really?"

"Can you get down, okay?" I ask. "Be careful."

"OW!" Miguel yelps. "He doesn't like being inside my shirt."

My hands are dripping sweat as I struggle to keep my eyes on the bottom of Miguel's sneakers. "Wait," I cry, as he's about to put his foot on a branch the width of my finger. "That's way too skinny. Try the one to the left. It's a lot stronger. Yes .... Yes, that one."

I don't realize I'm holding my breath until dark shapes swim in front of my eyes, and I take a deep gulp. I can see Miguel clearly now, about ten feet above my head. He stops and peers down at me. "Rylee? I'm gonna drop Oscar to you, okay?"

"What? No!"

"I have to. It's too hard to climb with him."

I bite my lip, terrified I'll drop him. "Um ... well, okay," I say, raising my arms.

Miguel pulls the kitten from his T-shirt and lowers his arm. "Ready?"

Oscar is squalling now, twisting his furry legs like he wants to punch somebody. "Ready," I say, even though I'm not at all ready. Then there's a heavy "thud" as Oscar lands in my outstretched hands, and I instinctively squeeze him against my chest. I can't believe I actually caught him. I stare into his furious little face and laugh with relief. "OMG! Hi, Oscar. Hi, boy."

"Oscar!" Melanie squeals, running over. And I hand her the kitten with a rush of pride. "See, Melanie. I told you he'd be okay. Don't let him go now. Careful."

Miguel lands on his feet beside us a few seconds later. "Whoo!" he says, grinning. His glasses sit crooked on his face, and he looks like a scarecrow with all the twigs and leaves sticking out of his hair. "Mission accomplished." He holds up his hand for a high five and I slap it hard. "Nice job!" I say. "Nice hair-do too."

He bends over and gives his hair a vigorous rub. "Any better?"

"Not much," I say, laughing.

Margo limps over and throws her arms around him. "That was amazing. How can I ever thank you? You're the best." She lets him go so she can hug me. "Both you kids. Talk about a fantastic team."

"You're welcome," I say, laughing. "But Miguel did all the hard work."

"Yeah, but you made a great coach," Miguel says. "It's like a jungle up there." He takes off his glasses and tries to clean them with the bottom of his T-shirt.

Melanie is smiling as big as a little kid can smile, squeezing the daylights out of Oscar, until Margo swoops both of them up into her arms. "What do you say to Rylee and Miguel, Melanie? They rescued your kitty. What do you say?"

"Thank you," she says on command.

"Wait right here," Margo tells us. "I've got sodas in the fridge for you two."

A few minutes later, Miguel and I are on our way again, sipping our pop like nothing ever happened. "Well," Miguel says. "That was fun."

I giggle. "Yeah, only because you didn't end up breaking your neck." I glance at my phone. "And amazingly enough, the incredible kitten caper took under fifteen minutes."

Miguel's eyebrows shoot up. "Hmm, the incredible kitten caper—great title for a story, don't you think?"

I laugh. "Not bad."

We walk the next block in silence, and I keep reliving Oscar's rescue—how cool the whole thing was. Not quite as cool as the day Thomas got rescued, of course, but still, I really admire Miguel for being willing to help a little kid. And I love the way Melanie's mom acted like it was such a huge deal, how she called us a fantastic team. It makes me think of Miguel's advice to give Anastar a sidekick, a best bud—and I'm ready to admit that maybe he's right. Maybe it's exactly what my story needs.

Miguel drains the last of his soda and tosses the can in the garbage as we pass Dairy Depot. "Busy this afternoon?" he asks.

"Why?" I ask, smiling. "Does somebody else need rescuing?"

"Naw. Just wondered if you might wanna see my clandestine writing spot?"

I pause. My gut reaction is to say no, but only because I'm scared to say yes. If I agree to go, am I agreeing to be real friends? My chest starts to squeeze, and my heart goes all fluttery like I'm facing some huge, life changing decision. "What makes it so clandestine?" I ask, stalling for time.

He smiles. "I dunno. It's quiet, hidden away. Mostly I just like the word."

And that's when it hits me. *Quiet? Hidden away?* Sounds like the perfect spot to train Coco? I feel an urgent need to see this place. And using Coco for a reason makes it less scary. "Is it okay if I bring my dog?"

Miguel's chin shoots up, like he's startled I'm agreeing to come. "Sweet," he says. "I love dogs."

"She's a puggle," I say. "Super cute and kinda wild."

He hoots. "A puggle? Sounds like a cross between a poodle and a mud puddle."

I laugh. "Good one, but no. Beagle and pug."

"Cool," he says. "I can wait for you at the corner if you wanna go home and get her right now."

"It will take me at least fifteen minutes."

"No problem," he says. "I'll wait."

"Okay," I agree. "I'll try to be fast."

I split for home as soon as we reach the corner, but I only make it a block before the second guessing takes over. What in the world am I doing? What if it's a huge mistake? I can't do it. My throat starts to close and my whole body goes tingly. I slow down to catch my breath and grope for the squeezie ball in my pocket.

But a few seconds later, my fear turns to anger. What is wrong with me? Why can't I just be normal instead of being terrified of things that aren't even scary? "You *can* do this," I say out loud. "You are not gonna stand up Miguel. You're just not."

As luck would have it, I walk into the house to discover Mom's taking a shower and Dad's busy with his occupational therapist. Perfect. I scrawl a quick note and slide it under the bathroom door. Then I grab my story notebook, because even though this really has nothing to do with writing, I have to pretend it does.

Coco bounces beside me like Tigger as I slip her harness over her head. "C'mon, girl," I whisper. "We're gonna go check out a new training spot." As soon as we step outside, she puts her nose to the ground and takes off like a bloodhound on a trail, twisting and pulling and almost tripping me.

Miguel is leaning up against a tree at the corner, playing on his phone while he waits. As soon as he sees us he tucks it in his pocket, drops on one knee and snaps his fingers at Coco. She acts shy for two heartbeats and then barrels into him, her tongue working overtime.

Miguel laughs and wipes slobber from his face. "Whoa, you're awesome. Look at your big feet. Wanna come live at my house for a while?"

I toss him the leash with a smile. "Nope, she doesn't. But you can borrow her right now."

We make our way to the lavish, Victorian style Chateau Saint Michelle winery and slip around back. There are a few people hanging out near the tasting room, but they don't pay us any attention as Miguel leads the way to a secluded fenced area at the far end of the rolling lawn. We slip through an unlocked wooden gate into a grassy alcove with a picnic table and a padlocked storage shed hidden beneath a huge weeping willow.

"Hey, check it out," I quip, "another willow. Hope there's no kitten." But I get right away why he calls the place clandestine, and I can barely contain my excitement. It's the perfect spot to work with Coco. Now all I have to do is figure out a time when we can be here alone without Miguel.

He gestures to the storage shed. "It's for the maintenance people, but I never see anybody back here."

I shade my eyes with a hand and take in the endless rows of vines, loaded with fat, purple grapes, and the mounded blue hills in the distance. "Those hills are so pretty."

"They're called the Horse Heavens," Miguel says. "Sweet name, huh?"

"Are there really horses up there?"

"Used to be, lots of wild mustangs. Now it's farmland."

I nod. "It's so peaceful here. How did you find it?"

Miguel scoots up his glasses and points off past my head. "You can't really see it unless you know where to look, but my house is about a quarter mile past that big cherry orchard."

I follow his pointing finger and think back to the day of the fire, trying to find some kind of familiar landmark. If his house is that direction, Uncle Gus's must be nearby too. But all I can see from here are trees, and I've never figured out east and west and all that stuff anyway. "So, you just stumbled across it one day, or what?"

"Naw, my brother Alex found it when he was ten. I was only seven, but he promised to show me if I didn't tell Mom. We weren't supposed to ride this far on our bikes, but we used to play here all the time."

"So Alex must be the one Thomas belongs to?"

"Yep." He steps over to the willow and gently swipes his fingertips over the trunk like he's spreading butter. "Alex was big into carving."

I edge closer to see all the letters etched into the smooth bark. "That's a lot of initials."

Miguel sniffs. "I know, right? A.G. is for Alex. M.G. is me. D.W. was his best friend Danny. My parents' initials are on the other side." He points higher. "See that word way up there? It took him like two hours to carve it. I remember, because I was starving that day. I wanted to go home but he made me stay until he finished."

I recall Miguel's comment about him and his brother climbing trees, and I tip my head back and squint at the word. "Pokémon?"

"Yeah. He was a big fan." He smiles up at the carving likes it's an old friend before turning back to me. "You can wedge Coco's leash under one of the table legs if you're worried about her running off."

"Oh, good idea," I say. Coco seems offended after finding herself tied, but ten seconds later she sprawls on her side in the shade.

Miguel laughs. "Guess she's tired."

"She should be," I say. "She ran all the way here." I perch on the bench and swing my legs over "So, do you usually come here after school?"

Miguel plops down across from me. "Depends."

"On what?"

"What else I've got going."

"How about weekends?"

"Sometimes."

I bite my tongue. How am I supposed to find out when Coco and I can be here by ourselves?

"You like writing on paper?" he asks.

"What? Oh." I glance at my notebook, embarrassed. "Yeah, actually I do. Weird, huh?"

"No. Dad does some of his stuff long hand too. How's your dad doing?"

I force a smile. "Good, getting lots stronger. He can transfer from his bed to his wheelchair by himself now."

"Sweet." He wiggles his eyebrows. "And meanwhile on other planets, how's poor, lonely Anastar been?"

I clear my throat and try to think of a way to tell him I've decided to take his advice without admitting he was right. "I keep this list of cool character names," I say, "and one of them is Lucia. I've been thinking I might add a Lucia to the story."

Miguel's smile spreads from his mouth to his eyes. "As a sidekick for Anastar?"

I pretend to consider it. "Mmm … I dunno. Might work."

He looks so happy it's almost embarrassing. "Awesome. So are you gonna enter a chapter in the contest?"

"I'm still not sure," I say. I don't add that I've been so busy with Coco I've all but forgotten the contest. "What about you?"

"I'm in with a short story. It's about these two boys hiking Mount Rainier with their dad when a storm blows in and traps them."

"Sounds exciting."

"Yeah." He tips his hand back and forth. "It's kinda based on real life."

"You've hiked Mount Rainier?"

"Naw, it's still on my bucket list. But this one time, Alex and I were hiking with Dad in the Wenatchee National Forest, and Dad fell and broke his ankle. No cell reception, of course, so he sent us back to the truck to call for help. It was like two miles."

"How old were you?"

"Six."

"So Alex was ... nine? Wow. Were you scared?"

Miguel snorts. "Not to start with. But Alex thought for sure we were gonna run into a grizzly on the way back. He got me so petrified I about peed my pants."

I laugh. Coco raises her head and fixes me with a worried expression until I reach down to rub her ears. "So the kids in the story are really you and your brother. You just changed the setting."

"Pretty much. Dad says authors do that a lot, write themselves into their own stories."

I consider this. Anastar is some like me. And she wants to save her mom, like I want to save Dad. "Interesting," I muse. "So, if your brother's three years older he must be a ninth grader now?"

Miguel releases a soft breath before he answers. "He would've been," he says. "But he died two years ago."

His words punch me in the chest, and for a moment I'm speechless. "What! Oh, gosh, Miguel ... what happened?"

He digs at a small fleck of paint on the picnic table with his thumbnail. "Brain tumor," he says simply.

"Oh … Wow. I'm so sorry."

"Thanks," he says. "It's why I come here. It's where I remember him best."

Shame oozes through me, and I feel like a big, fat slug for planning to ditch him and steal this place for myself. "Why did you bring me here?" I can't help but ask.

He seems puzzled by the question. "Cause it's a great place to write, and you like to write … right?" He smiles.

"Right," I say. "But if it reminds you so much of Alex, don't you wanna keep it for yourself?"

"I have," he admits, "for two years. I guess I'm a little tired of keeping it to myself." He raises his eyebrows and offers a goofy grin, like he's trying to joke over his sadness. "Besides, sharing's supposed to be a good thing. Or so my mom tells me."

That word *sharing* is all it takes to make my throat tighten and pins and needles spark through my body. I start digging at my own fleck of paint as my memories take over.

CHAPTER THIRTEEN

IFTH GRADE HAS *ended and it's the first Friday of summer vacation. I am so disappointed that your cousin Carla is visiting from Texas and you're busy. But then you call at five o'clock. "We're bored," you say. "Come to the overpass with us."*

I haven't had a panic attack for many months, but my throat instantly thickens and my chest gets tight. "Don't take her to the overpass," I say.

"Why not?" you ask.

I am stunned by your question. "Because it's our special spot. You can't take her there."

"She's only here until Sunday," you say, "then she's going back home."

"Good," I say. "We'll go as soon as she leaves."

You make a scoffing sound in the back of your throat. "Mom says I have to entertain her. We've already straightened our hair and baked cookies and watched TV. She wants to see the overpass."

"So what. Take her somewhere else."

"It's a public place," you say, sounding confused. "It's not like it will change anything."

My heart thuds in my chest, because you don't understand that it will. It will change so much. You are my *best friend. The overpass is* our *special place. It's where we cemented our friendship and made our pledge. It can't be shared with anyone else. How can you not get that?*

"Come with us, please?" you say. "I need you."

I grit my teeth. "Carla's not nice to me," I say, "she's obnoxious. She's not even nice to you."

"I know," you admit. "That's why I want you to come. She's not near as wild when there's another person around."

"No," I say.

"Pleeeeease," you beg, and I start to waver. But then I remember how Carla taunted me for being afraid to dive off the low dive at the city swimming pool, how she wrinkled her nose and smirked. How I wanted so badly to say something mean to her but was too afraid. And I can't bear to think of her rubbing her hand along the steel safety rail of the overpass, sitting on our bench, laughing… with you. "I can't," I say. "I'm busy."

"Doing what?" you ask, and now I hear the anger in your voice.

"Dad's taking us to Gunning's Alley for pizza when he gets home from work."

A long pause. A pause full of suspicion. "Why didn't you tell me that before?" you ask.

"Because I just remembered now."

"Fine," you say. "Whatever."

"Whatever," I snap back. And I hang up. I'm not sure why I hang up. I know even as I do it's wrong, and I'm ashamed of myself. I want to call you back. But my blood is boiling, and my throat is nearly closed. If you're going to betray me, if you're going to take Carla to the overpass, you deserve to be hung up on.

I don't call you back. I start to cry instead.

CHAPTER FOURTEEN

THE "SCRITCH-SCRITCH" OF fingernail on wood pulls me back to the present, and I realize the sound is coming from Miguel's thumb. Mine is stiff, hovering an inch above the picnic table like it's forgotten how to flex. I can't remember the last thing Miguel said, but it doesn't really matter. What matters is that I'm a petty, jealous person and he's not. I wish I was more like him. I especially wish I'd been more like him the night I refused to go with Molly. I'd just been so sure that if she took Carla to the overpass, it would somehow make it not special anymore. That it would damage our friendship—maybe even ruin it forever. And strangely enough, it had.

I reach down to touch Coco, to reassure myself she's still there. She is, of course, and I'm so glad I have her. But suddenly, she's not enough. And I realize how much I miss Molly. How much I miss having a real friend to share special things with. I twirl a strand of hair around my finger and yank until it hurts. "I haven't been writing much lately," I admit to Miguel. "I've had another project going on."

His thumb goes still and he glances over. "Yeah?"

My resolve wavers for a few seconds, like a teeter totter balancing between the freedom of the air and the hard crash of the ground. I'm scared of what might happen if I tell him more. But I'm even more scared of letting my fear win. It's been doing that a lot lately—controlling me instead of the other way around—and I know it's not the way things should be. I wipe my palms on my jeans. "I've been working a lot with Coco. Training her to do special things."

"Like what?"

"Things like ... well, do you know what you're supposed to do if your clothes catch on fire?"

Miguel's shoulders jump back and he laughs. "If my clothes ... what, you mean besides jump around and scream?" But then he realizes I'm not laughing with him and he straightens his face. "Oh, you're for real. Um, okay, let's see. You're *not* supposed to jump around and scream, you're supposed to lay down and roll to smother the fire ... right?"

"Exactly," I say. "Stop, drop and roll. Coco can do that."

Miguel holds my gaze for a few seconds before glancing down at Coco. He cocks an eyebrow. "No way."

"Yes way."

"Show me."

I gesture toward his backpack. "Got any food?"

"What kind of food?" He tugs open the zipper and rummages around. "Some bread crusts from my sandwich?"

"Good enough." I nudge Coco with my toe. "Wake up, girl. It's time to work. Want a treat?"

She blinks sleepy eyes at the nudge, but as soon as I say *treat*, she springs to life.

Miguel grins. "She knows that word."

I grin back proudly. "She knows a lot of words," I say. "But that one's still her favorite." I close the bread crusts in my fist and wave them under Coco's nose. I lead her away from the picnic table, put her in a sit and then take several steps back. She watches unblinking, her eyes focused on the hand with the treats. "Come," I say, hoping the slight shakiness in my voice doesn't unnerve her. As soon as she moves toward me, I raise my palm. "Stop."

She immediately halts, waits for me to lower my hand toward the ground, then lays down and rolls over, her pudgy legs waving in the air. "Good girl," I cry, holding out a bite of bread. "Good job."

Miguel claps. "Wow, sweet!"

I beam, so excited I'm lightheaded. "I know, right?"

"Do it again," he says.

So we do, twice more, and then I sweep low in a bow as Miguel whistles. "Thank you," I say. "Thank you very much."

"Awesome," he says. "What else can she do?"

"That's as far as we've gotten. But I'm gonna teach her to crawl next because it's what you do if you're surrounded by smoke and you're trying to find an exit."

"But how do you teach a dog something like that?"

I raise my hands. "Good question. But I'll show you what I'm gonna try." I pull out my phone, find the YouTube video and hand it to Miguel. He watches it while I fasten Coco's leash back to the picnic table and sit down.

"So cool," he says, handing back the phone with a thoughtful look, and I brace for what I know is coming next. "Are you teaching her that stuff just for the fun of it?"

"No." I clear my throat and think how best to explain. Because even though it's scary, I *do* want to explain. I want to trust Miguel with something important, like he did me. "I told you my dad's a fireman," I begin. "He's always been. It's what he loves most, next to Mom and me. But ever since the accident... he's changed a lot. We used to do stuff together all the time, you know? But now he's not that way. It's almost like . . ." I drop my voice low, as if a quiet voice will make the words hurt less. ". . . like he doesn't want to be my dad anymore."

Miguel scoots up his glasses and nods, as if he understands.

"So, anyway . . ." I continue. "My uncle Gus and I talked one day, about Dad still being a fireman even though he can't do a lot of the physical stuff anymore.

How he could maybe be involved in the training and education part of it. You know, like teaching school kids and maybe even new firefighters. And I got this idea that if I could train Coco to be his partner, then maybe he'd see that he can still do what he loves, and he'd be willing to try."

"Well, shoot," Miguel says, "if he doesn't want to, I'll do it."

I smile, because I didn't expect that, and it fills me with new confidence. If Miguel believes in my idea enough to volunteer himself, then it must be an idea worth believing in. And without any warning at all my eyes turn blurry, because I realize how badly I need somebody to believe in my plan, to believe in me. I lean down to pet Coco again, blinking fast.

"Does your uncle know about your plan?" Miguel asks.

I sit back up. "Nope. I only promised to teach her something useful to a fireman so he'd let me keep her." I explain how Coco turned up at the fire station, and how Mom's not so crazy about dogs. "I'm afraid if my parents knew my plan they'd think it was more like a joke," I admit.

"Well, you're gonna have the last laugh," Miguel says, grinning. "When are you gonna tell them?"

The question gives me pause. "I dunno," I say. "There's still a lot more I need to teach her. But it's tough to work with her at home without anybody seeing. I've been trying to find, you know... a more clandestine spot."

Miguel smiles. Then a few seconds later his chin lifts, and I watch realization creep into his face. "Oh," he says, sounding self-conscious. "Like here. That's why you agreed to come."

"Only at first," I hurriedly explain. "But now I understand about your brother. I know this place is special to you."

"It's okay," he says. "Now I know about your plan too. We both learned something new. Mr. Hinkle would be proud."

I giggle and throw my arms wide. "Yeah, right, all this is so scientific."

There is a sudden low roar overhead, and we both crane our necks to see the black dot of a jet far above. I watch its chalky white contrail turn wide and feathery before it slowly becomes part of the blue sky. Then I take a deep breath of the fruity air and glance at Miguel. "Soooo, would you mind if I came here to work with Coco? And maybe to work on my book some too? I won't tell anybody else about it."

He shrugs. "I don't mind," he says. "As long as you don't mind if I'm here sometimes too. But if either one of us minds, it will ruin things for both of us."

I laugh. "That was the most confusing thing I ever heard. But yeah, sure."

"Need any help?" he asks.

I tip my head. "Help?"

"With Coco? Training her."

My muscles tense, and the word *No* instantly bubbles up in my throat. Coco is *my* dog. Training her is *my* project. *My* surprise. But then I look into Miguel's eager eyes and feel a horrible sinking sensation. Despite all the awful stuff that's happened in the past three months, I haven't changed at all. I'm still selfish, still afraid to share. And the worst part is, I'm not sure I know how to fix myself. But maybe it wouldn't hurt to try.

"Why not?" I say, smiling. "Even Superman needed Lois Lane."

HAPTER FIFTEEN

OM AND DAD are sitting on the porch drinking coffee when Coco and I get home. Mom's laptop is perched on the wicker table between them, and I can tell something's up by the way they're hunched together studying it.

"Hey," I say.

They both glance up. "Hey, girl," Dad says. "Have a ood walk?"

"I hope you didn't go far," Mom adds.

I figure the winery might be a little past what she considers far. "I didn't," I say. "It was good." I unsnap Coco's leash and rub her head. "Coco sure could use some leash raining, though." She raises her ears and tips her head like he gets the joke, and I have to bite my lip to keep from racking up. I squat beside Dad's wheelchair. "What are ou guys looking at?"

"A job site Diane told me about during therapy," he says.

It takes a few seconds for the meaning of his words to reach my brain. But when they do, I feel a crushy sensation in my chest. "A job site?" I echo, trying to keep my voice steady.

"Yeah," Dad says, like he's trying not to laugh. "Jobs. Ever hear of 'em?"

I swallow. "Yeah … of course. But I mean, like what kind? Firefighting jobs?"

Dad winces.

Mom cements her lips together like I've spouted a four letter word.

My question twists in the air, dark and scary, like some poisonous thing about to bite.

"No," Dad says quietly. "Jobs that I can do. So I can provide for you guys."

It feels like all the air has been sucked from my lungs.

Mom stares me down, daring me to say anything more.

I steady myself on Dad's chair as I stand. "I gotta get a drink. Anybody want anything?" I slip through the slider without waiting for an answer and make a bee line for the kitchen sink. I fill a tall glass with water, force a few sips down, and then creep back over to the window by the slider. I separate the mini blinds just enough to peek through. A reflection blocks most of Mom's laptop, but I can just make out the top third of the screen.

Welcome to disABLEperson.com—a Premier Job Board for People with Disabilities since 2002.

I sink into a kitchen chair and choke down another swallow of water. There's actually a job site just for disabled people. And Dad's looking at it. My teeth start to ache. I pull out my phone, call up the site and scroll through the job categories.

Insurance	*Law*
Banking	*Hospitality*
Manufacturing	*Real-estate*

Despair whooshes through me and makes me dizzy, and I can't bear to see any more. I stumble down the hall, snag a squeezie ball, and flop on my air mattress. Then I close my eyes and focus on breathing as I squeeze and release. Back in second grade a school nurse told me that calm breathing can help you float right through your worry or panic. In through the nose to a count of three, out through the mouth to a count of three. The rhythm feels good, but it doesn't take my mind off Dad.

He can't be looking at other jobs—he *has* to stay a fireman. How in the world can Coco be useful to him if he's a banker or a real estate agent? My jaw burns, and I've lost count of my breathing. I pinch the bridge of my nose to keep from crying.

Mom opens my door a few minutes later and I jerk upright. She's normally pretty good about knocking, but not this time, and I'm caught dead to rights with the squeezie ball. I can feel her worry as she stares at my hand. "When did you start using those again?" she asks quietly.

Shame splashes over me as our eyes meet. I release the ball and let it fall beside me. "I haven't been," I say, shrugging. "Not much anyway. It was just ... lying there is all."

"Mmm," she says, then sighs. "Well, come peel some potatoes for me, please."

"Yeah, okay."

But instead of leaving like I expect her to, she steps into my room and nudges the door closed with her heel. "What's wrong, honey?"

I try to look confused, which isn't much of a stretch right then. "Nothing. I'll be out in a minute."

"Why did you act so surprised when Dad mentioned the job site?"

I swallow. I do not want to have this conversation right now, not when I still feel woozy. "I didn't."

"Yeah, you did. You seemed stunned, in fact. Why, Rylee?"

The last thing I want to do is cry, but my eyes blur anyway and I swipe at them. "I didn't get ... why, is all."

"Why, what?"

"Dad's a fireman," I say, my voice hushed. "What other jobs is he searching?"

Mom closes her eyes for several seconds. Then she steps over and kneels on the rug in front of me. She studies my face. "Dad *was* a fireman, honey. Things have changed."

I grit my teeth. "He still is one," I insist. "He's on Fire Nation all the time—the website, and the chatroom. I see him, Mom. He binge watches L.A. Firefighters, and he's always asking Uncle Gus what's going on at work. And he keeps in touch with the guys in Elliott Bay too."

Mom's shoulders slump. "Of course he does all that. He still loves it. He misses it. Firefighting's in his blood. But look at him, honey. He's ... paralyzed," she adds, as if it's a point I may have somehow missed over the past three months. "But now he's healed to the point where he's starting to consider the future. How he can go back to work again."

I nod. "Yeah, I know but . . ."

"Wait," Mom holds up a finger. "I'm not done yet. Now, I know you love the fact that your dad's a fireman. You've always been so proud of him and I totally get it. But honey, Dad's firefighting days are behind him. He knows that. But he'll have a much easier time accepting it if we do."

"But there's other jobs he could still do tied in with firefighting," I say. "Uncle Gus even said so." The last five words slip out before I can stop them.

Mom draws back. "What are you talking about?"

"Uncle Gus says Dad could maybe do education work for the fire department. You know, teaching, public relations type stuff."

She seems to consider this for a moment. "That may be true," she says. "But any job he gets will have to be a desk job, Rylee. What difference does it make if it's with the fire department or something else? It's all the same."

My nose burns as fresh tears fill my eyes. How can she be so clueless about something so important? "No, it's not all the same," I say, like I'm explaining something to a kindergartner. "Not even close. If he works for the fire department, he'll still be a fireman. You know it's what he wants."

Mom shakes her head and sighs, like I'm the clueless one. "Our job, at this point, is to be as supportive as we can, Rylee. To encourage him and make sure he knows we'll stand behind him no matter what choice he makes."

The frustration is building in my chest and I wave my hands. "But what other choice would he make?"

"Actually," she says, "he's considering an online accounting course."

I freeze, as my heart cracks. I don't trust myself to speak. "A-accounting?" I whisper. "He'd be bored to death. He'd hate it."

Mom drops her gaze to the floor, and I know she's so disappointed in me. "You might hate it," she says. "But that doesn't mean he would."

My heart's so heavy I expect it to drop out onto the mattress beside me. Mom places a hand over mine. "Why does it matter so much to you that he's still a fireman? Talk to me, honey."

Her question makes me sick inside, because it's almost word for word what Uncle Gus asked. It's like the two of them are plotting against me. But I have no better answer for her than for him. "Because," I say, "I just want him to be happy." But as the words slip from my lips, I'm surprised by how fake and rehearsed they sound, almost like I recorded them ahead of time.

"Do you?" Mom asks, her tone suddenly sharper. "Do you really? Because if that's true, you won't ever again say anything to him about being a fireman. He's got enough of a load to carry without us adding to it."

Mom finally leaves, and I sag across my mattress feeling way more lost than before she came in. *Never say anything to him again about being a fireman?* She has no idea what she's asking. If Dad's not a fireman, he'll never be happy. I'll never be happy. It's the only thing that will ever bring us back together again, the only way I have of giving back what I helped take away from him.

I go to bed at ten that night, but I don't go to sleep. I lay wide awake until Uncle Gus's key finally turns in the lock. Then I inch away from Coco and pad out to the kitchen. Uncle Gus is peering into the opened refrigerator, his face bathed in bright light. "Hey, Uncle Gus."

He startles. "Whoa there, girl! What are you doing up, it's almost midnight?"

"I need to talk to you."

He grabs the milk jug and lets the refrigerator close. "Can it wait until morning? I'm pretty bushed."

"Not really," I say. "But it won't take long, promise."

He pours himself a glass of milk, takes a long swig and wipes a hand across his moustache. "Okay then. Let's go upstairs so we don't wake your folks."

I trail him upstairs, which is now his main living area thanks to us. He flips on a lamp and sinks into his leather recliner. "So what's up?"

I fidget before him, trying to choose my words. Then I decide this is one of those times when it's best to blurt it straight out for the shock value. "Dad wants to take an online accounting course."

Uncle Gus cocks an eyebrow. "Accounting?"

"Yeah," I say, disappointed by his lack of reaction. "Is that insane or what?"

"Well, surprising maybe. I dunno about insane. He's always been a whiz with numbers."

I twist my hands and perch on the edge of the sofa across from him. "But honestly, think about it, Uncle Gus. Can you really see Dad sitting at a desk in front of a calculator all day, every day?"

"You have something against accountants?" he asks, smiling.

I don't smile back. "Diane showed him this website with job listings for disabled people. He and Mom were looking at it earlier."

He takes another swallow of milk before nodding. "So he's moving ahead. That's a good thing."

"No it's not," I say. "Not if he's gonna go and do something crazy like become an accountant."

"What does your mom think?"

The question sends irritation surging through me. I want to rudely remind him we're not talking about Mom, but I decide that switching directions is probably the better strategy. "Did you check into the fireman education idea we talked about?"

Uncle Gus drains the rest of his milk. Then he sets the glass on the end table harder than necessary and fixes me with a look. "Even if I could make something like that happen, and I'm not saying I could, it's still too soon. Your dad's not ready. He's still doing therapy several times a week."

"But he's checking out jobs."

"There's a world of difference between taking online classes at home, and going to a job each day. He'd need to be able to do a lot more by himself, including driving. And speaking of driving, he'd need a specially equipped vehicle too. And that's only a start."

I swallow. Dad's come a long way in the past several weeks. He's not having as much problem with muscle spasms. He can dress himself and transfer back and forth between his chair and other places. He can maneuver his chair any place it will fit, and he can get himself up and down the outdoor ramp without help. But driving? Well, I hadn't thought of that. "He could go with you," I say. "Or Mom could drive him back and forth."

Uncle Gus frowns. "Did you ever think your mom might like her own life back again? Maybe go back to work herself? I doubt she wants to be a chauffeur the rest of her life."

The pressure is building in my chest again, and I wish I had one of my squeezie balls. "Okay," I admit. "So we'd have to work some more stuff out first. But it *is* a possibility, right?"

"Answer my question first."

I blink. "What question?"

"What does your mom think?"

My nose stings like it has vinegar in it. Of all people, I expected Uncle Gus to understand, to be on my side. Do not cry, I command myself. Be strong. Be a dandelion. "She thinks I should be supportive," I say, putting a sarcastic twist on the last word.

He leans toward me, his palms flat on his knees. "She's right, you know?"

I grit my teeth. "Just tell me, Uncle Gus... please. Is a job with the fire department a possibility?"

"Yeah," he says. "It's a possibility. I told you before."

My relief comes out in a noisy whoosh. "Okay, then can you please, please tell him that before he goes and does something he'll hate?"

Uncle Gus seems to be gazing through me, his eyes full of the same doubt I saw in Mom's. And I can't stand them for not getting it. For acting like I'm a terrible person for wanting Dad to stay a firefighter—like I'm somehow trying to *keep* him from being happy, when the very opposite is true. There's so much pressure in my chest I'm afraid it's going to explode if I don't jump around or holler or do something to give it release. But I dig my fingernails into my palms and manage to stay still until Uncle Gus meets my eyes a moment later. "You know, Rylee," he says, "just because something's a possibility, doesn't mean it's right for your dad."

My shoulders droop, and my fight fizzles away. It's not only a letdown, it's a flat out betrayal. "But it *is*," I say. "It is the right thing, Uncle Gus. Please ... just think about telling him."

He nods. "You think about it too," he says.

And I say nothing, because I'm not even sure what he means. All I know is that I feel as withered and empty as a popped balloon. I creep back to bed and nestle against Coco. She's soft and warm and smells of grass. But even she can't stop the awful sensation of my plan slipping through my fingers like wet soap.

CHAPTER SIXTEEN

"HAVE A COOKIE," Miguel says, holding it out to me across the picnic table. "Maybe it'll help you think."

I glance up from my story notebook with a fake scowl. "How do you know I need help thinking?"

He grins. "You've been staring at the same page for ten minutes."

"You've been timing me?"

"Okay, maybe not ten minutes, but a long time."

I haven't been able to focus on much of anything the past few weeks, so I doubt a cookie's going to help, but it looks good anyway. "Fine," I say with a smile. "Give me the cookie." I focus back on my story as I nibble. "Okay, so Lucia and Anastar are at the rebel luminary base, but I have no idea how to get them inside to rescue her mom."

"Hmm," Miguel says. "A sneak attack, maybe? Explosives are always good."

I laugh. "This is a book, not a movie."

"You can use explosives in books."

"What I really want is something ... different. Something the reader doesn't expect."

"Ahh," Miguel says. "Surprise twists are good."

"I know," I say. "But not for the writer."

"Try reading your last chapter again," he suggests. "You know, what led up to that point. Maybe something will jump out at you."

I swallow a bite of cookie and check my phone. "It'll have to wait 'till later. I'm supposed to be home helping mom get ready for the party."

"What's it for again?" Miguel asks.

"To celebrate some big insurance payment. We're gonna use it to remodel the bathroom so Dad has more room to get around. It paid for his new wheelchair too."

"What's different about the chair?"

"Smaller and lighter. Easier for him to maneuver."

"The sports model, huh?"

"Yeah, something like that."

"Seems like a good enough reason for a party."

I sniff. The party's the last thing I want to talk about, but I force a smile anyway. "Mom's calling it the Going Ahead Gala, pretty lame, huh?"

"Sounds like a regular black tie affair."

"I know, right?" I offer Coco my last bite of cookie and she wolfs it down with tail wagging.

"Who all's coming?"

"Just a few of the guys Dad worked with in Elliott Bay, and their wives."

Miguel gives me a pointed look. "You're gonna show them what Coco can do, aren't you? It's the perfect time."

The question makes my heart hurt. But I shrug, like it's no big deal instead of the enormous thing it is. "It *would've* been the perfect time," I correct. "I'm not sure it even matters now."

"It matters," Miguel says. "You guys have worked too hard not to."

Coco stands and puts her front paws on my knee. She's probably just fishing for more cookie, but it feels like maybe she knows what we're talking about, and her happy face blurs before my eyes. She's so smart, and such a great student. Not only can she stop, drop and roll, but over the past three weeks Miguel and I have taught her to crawl and play dead. She's amazing, and she deserves to show off her skills—even if they never get used. Even if my whole wonderful plan has gone down the toilet like an ugly, useless turd.

I give another disheartened shrug. "I told you Dad started his accounting course last week. He talks about it like it's this great thing."

"It still matters," Miguel repeats, almost like he's scolding me. "Your dad will be really impressed when he sees what Coco can do. Especially when he finds out you did it for him. Shoot, maybe he'll be so impressed he'll forget all about accounting."

I think about telling him how much the course cost, so there's no way Dad's going to forget about it. But I know he's only trying to make me feel better, so I take a snuffly breath and force myself to nod. "Yeah, maybe," I say. "Will you come help me?"

His eyes get big. "Come to the party?"

"Why not, you're the co-trainer?" I smile at Coco. "What do you think, girl? Should Miguel come too?" She licks my hand and her tail sways. "See," I say. "Coco thinks it's a great idea."

"But will your parents?"

I'm not sure about that one. All I know is, I'll be asking Coco to perform in front of her first real audience—an audience made up of people who either have no idea I've taught her anything, or who don't believe I could. I need Miguel for moral support. I'll be much braver if he's there. And even though I'm too embarrassed to admit it out loud, Melanie's mom was right—we are a fantastic team. I offer a reassuring smile as I swing my legs over the bench and gather Coco's leash. "They'll be fine with it," I say. "Text you tomorrow morning and let you know what time."

Miguel seems pleased. "Okay, sweet."

I amble home as slowly as Coco will allow, trying to focus on the beautiful golds and reds of the changing leaves instead of what the next day or two will bring. The weather's cooled some now, and Cayuse is full of trucks hauling wooden bins of Gala and Yellow Delicious apples. The air doesn't smell like grapes anymore, it smells like apple pie.

The irrigation canals are still swirling with murky brown water, and you can still hear the rhythmic *schick–schick–schick* of sprinklers squirting out their streams of water everywhere. Uncle Gus says Cayuse gets snow in winter, sometimes enough to cancel school, which would be super cool to experience. Plus, Miguel claims there are some great hills around for tubing or snowboarding, which would be an awesome change from Elliott Bay where it rains so much the sidewalks are covered with drowned worms.

I'm thinking that I own two pair of rain boots but no snow boots as I round the corner near home. Guilt pings me when I see a blue Subaru with Oregon plates parked in the driveway. Someone has shown up early, but I don't recognize the car. Must be a rental.

Dad's best friend Sam is coming, but he drives a candy red Mustang. I think Brian and Rita have a mini-van, which is hilarious because they don't even have kids. And I can't remember what Chuck and Sharon drive. We'll have fifteen people total for the barbecue tomorrow—well, sixteen counting Miguel—but only the seven from out of town will be spending the night. I hope Mom had the house clean enough before the early birds showed up so she's not mad at me.

I usher Coco inside the yard, latch the gate and unclip her leash. "Be a good girl," I tell her, "and you might get to stay inside with the company." I slick on some lip gloss as I trot across the lawn and quietly open the slider, hoping to get a peek at the visitors before they see me. But Coco pushes past before I can stop her. "Hey," I call. "Get back here."

The living room's empty, but Dad's voice drifts in from the kitchen. I manage to grab Coco's collar and straddle her between my legs right as she rounds the corner. "Hi," I say. "Sorry about her running in like..."

Then I get my first look at the people seated around the table. My voice disappears, and a sudden chill slams my chest. I release Coco and hug my arms around myself.

"Rylee," Dad says.

That's all he says, just my name, in a warning tone of voice. But I don't turn to him. It's Molly I can't take my eyes off. She's curled into her chair, looking smaller than the last time I saw her, her face so pale against her dark hair I almost don't recognize her. "Hey," she says, her voice barely loud enough to hear over the excited clicking of Coco's toenails on the linoleum.

I glower at Mom as tears prick my eyes. "You could've told me," I say.

Guilt clouds her face, and she pauses long enough to tuck a lock of hair behind her ear. "Maybe I should have, but I knew what you'd say. And enough is enough."

"It's so good to see you, sweetie," Molly's mom Karen cuts in, her voice soft and hopeful.

I make myself glance at her. She has the same blue frame glasses, the same chin length hair—a shade darker than blond, with a wide strip of gray running through the middle. "Hi," I murmur.

"Is that your dog?" she asks. "She's adorable."

I glance at Coco without seeing her and nod.

Karen twists her thumb ring. "I'm sorry to catch you so much by surprise," she says. "But your parents and I think it's time for you girls to talk."

"Yep," Dad says. "So why don't you go sit out back and do that very thing."

My legs are rubber, and my jaw aches. I'm not sure what to do. The last thing I want is to talk to Molly. But Dad's words were a statement and not a suggestion, and I know I'm trapped. The injustice of it all makes me want to explode. I wheel around and dash back out the slider, then I drop down on the porch steps and bury my face in my knees.

I don't hear Molly come through the door, she's always had the ability to move like a cat. Or maybe it's just that my heart is thrumming like the bass on the car that often drives past. But I feel her sit beside me though, hear her short, anxious breaths. I lean away. "Who invited you?" I demand.

"Nobody," Molly says. "Mom read about the party on your mom's Facebook page. She asked if we could come."

And Mom said yes, I think. Big surprise. A fly buzzes my head and I resist the urge to bat it.

"I know you don't want me here," Molly says. "And you don't have to talk to me. Just listen, okay? Please . . . just listen."

A wet nose pokes my arm as Coco forces her way in between us, and I gratefully scoot aside and wrap an arm around her.

"She's so soft," Molly says. "Rocky's kind of wiry. We still have him, you know."

Her attempt at small talk sends anger raging through me. "It's only been three months. Why wouldn't you have him?"

"Because he got hit by a car last month and needed 36 stitches in his hip. He almost died."

For a moment I'm startled. I picture Rocky's black schnauzer face, his gentle chocolate eyes. We used to pretend he was half my dog, something else Molly and I shared. But I don't have any words of comfort right now. I feel more like hurting and punishing. "Gee," I say, snorting, "sounds a lot like someone else I know."

Molly winces, and I watch from the corner of my eye as the color drains from her already pale face. Then her shoulders hunch and she starts to cry.

Something inside me loosens, and I can't believe what I just said. I've never thought of myself as a cruel person, but I guess I am one now. If only there was some way to hear what your words will sound like before you actually say them. I throw a nervous look toward the house, hoping none of the adults come out to make an incredibly awkward situation even worse. "I'm sorry," I say. "I didn't mean it like that."

"Yeah, you did," Molly says. She wipes her eyes with the heel of her hand. She's wearing a dark blue Adidas T-shirt with big wet patches under the arms. It's not hot. She must be every bit as anxious as me. She swallows. "I wish it had been me who'd gotten hurt instead of your dad, Rylee. It's all I've thought about since it happened."

Me too, I think. But I bite my tongue, afraid anything I say might make her cry more.

"When you called me that day, after the police showed you the pictures," she continues, "I wanted to tell you the whole story right then, but I couldn't. I couldn't tell you anything because our lawyer said not to."

I'm not sure why the word lawyer surprises me, but it does. "You had a lawyer?"

"Yeah. And he said you aren't supposed to talk about a case while it's being investigated. Not to anybody. But I can tell you now, okay? So please ... just listen."

Molly hugs herself. "It was super windy the day Carla and I went to the overpass," she begins, staring at Dad's wheel-chair ramp like she's talking to it and not me. "There were all these pebbles everywhere. We were standing at the rail, watching the traffic. But then Carla picked up a handful of pebbles. She said she wanted to see how good her aim was."

I picture Carla's wide face, the way she rolled her eyes at me for being afraid to dive, and my stomach cramps.

"She tried a bunch of times," Molly continues. "I don't think she ever hit anything, but I didn't watch. I hoped maybe if I ignored her, she'd get bored and we could go back home, so I went over and sat on the bench. I started to text you, to say you were right, I shouldn't have brought her there. But before I could finish, Carla took off. I didn't know what she was up to. I thought maybe she'd gone back down to leave, so I never sent you the text. I just put my phone away and went to find her. But then she met me on the stairs with this . . . this rock. This really big rock."

Coco startles me with a whimper, and I realize I'm squeezing her too hard. I loosen my grip.

"She . . . she set it up on the rail, hanging on to it with one hand, you know, and she was laughing. It made me so mad. I yelled at her to be careful, that the rock might accidentally fall. That's when she claimed she was gonna drop it, that it would be big enough to actually hit something. I didn't believe her. I thought she was just being dumb, you know, showing off like she likes to do.

But then she picked out this blue semi-truck. You should've seen her face, Rylee. It scared me so bad, because suddenly I was afraid she was serious. I didn't know what to do. I thought if I grabbed her arm she might lose her hold on the rock, so I—I grabbed her around the waist instead. I tried to pull her back from the rail, but she panicked.

She elbowed me right in the face. The rock slipped when she tried to shove me away ... and that was it, you know. That was it."

My teeth are clenched so hard the pain is shooting up my ear and across my scalp. And I'm desperate for her to stop talking, because I already know the rest of the story. I know the rock missed the truck and crashed through Dad's windshield instead, landing inches from his lap. A shudder passes through me, and Molly reaches over and lays her hand on my knee.

"I tried so hard to stop her," she whispers. "You might not believe me, but I did, Rylee. I swear to you. But then it happened, and we both freaked out and ran. Carla told me we had to keep our mouths shut or we'd both go to jail. So I did, until the next day, until we found out it was ... your dad. But Carla was leaving the next morning. So I waited until we took her to the airport, and then as soon as she got on the plane, I told Mom what happened."

My head is swimming and Coco's the only thing that keeps me from toppling off the steps. "What did she say?"

"We went to the police. And they told us we'd better talk to a lawyer. So we did."

"What about Carla?"

"She told the police she never meant to drop the rock. That if I hadn't grabbed her, it wouldn't have happened."

I meet Molly's eyes for the first time. "Are you kidding me? She blamed you?"

Molly nods. "Pretty much, yeah. And the saddest part..." she pauses to take a raggedy breath. "I'm pretty sure she was telling the truth about not meaning to do it."

I stare at her, unable to wrap my mind around this. "Why would you believe her?"

"Because Carla's always been a show off. She likes to do risky stuff to get attention and impress people. But she's not a bad person, not really. She'd never hurt somebody on purpose."

I'm not convinced at all, but I don't say anything. Instead, I close my eyes and give my brain a moment to quit spinning. "So who did the police believe?"

"Me," Molly says, and there's a world of relief in that one word. "Carla and her parents came back to Oregon so we could have a hearing in front of a judge. And I was so scared, Rylee, because when you see the regular video from the highway cam, it's kind of hard to tell exactly what's going on, it's a little blurry and grainy. But at the courthouse they have this machine that slows down the camera, shows it frame by frame, kind of like in slow motion. And after the judge watched it, she said Carla was the responsible one. That even if she didn't plan to drop the rock, it was reckless and negligent of her to bring it up there in the first place, and especially to set it up on the rail like she did."

My heart speeds up. "So what happened? What did the judge do to her?"

"She sentenced her to this special program for kids who have never been in trouble with the police before. I don't remember the name of it, but she has to put in 200 hours of community service. And if she completes it all like she's supposed to then they'll take the charges off her record. But if she doesn't, she has to serve time in juvenile detention."

I think about this. Two hundred hours of community service. That's it? If she did five hours a day it would take only forty days. A joke compared to what she did to Dad, but still … it's something. And for the first time I wonder what Carla's life has been like since the accident. Does she regret it every day? Does she wake up with nightmares? "Have you talked to her since then?" I ask.

"No," Molly says. "I can't … yet. Maybe after a year or something, I'll be ready."

"Yeah," I say. My stomach's jelly, and my head weighs a thousand pounds, but strangely enough, I feel calm. I rest my head on my knees. So that's what Molly wanted so badly to tell me. It really *was* an accident—a stupid, reckless, needless one—but still, an accident. And she'd done her best to prevent it.

"Do my parents know all this?" I ask.

Molly nods. "As soon as the lawyer said it was okay to talk about it, Mom called your mom. But I didn't want you to hear it from her. I wanted to tell you. So Mom asked her not to say anything."

"When did the lawyer say you could talk about it?"

"The day I called you on Kara's phone."

I nod, numbly. I can't believe my parents could keep something like that from me. But then I think about the times Mom tried to bring the subject up, how I always cut her off. Maybe she did try to tell me.

"I know what you're thinking," Molly says, her voice heavy with sadness. "And you're right. I should've found *some* way to stop her. Believe me, Rylee, I think about it every single day, what I could've done different. I stay awake at night thinking about it. I've lost six pounds since it happened. Mom made me go to the doctor."

The selfish part of me wants to let her go right on believing what she believes, that it was her responsibility to prevent what happened. But there's a bigger part of me that's ready to comfort her, to share the truth like a real friend would do. I close my eyes for a few seconds to gather courage. "No," I admit, softly. "It's not what I'm thinking."

Molly turns and studies me with half closed eyes, like she doesn't have the strength to keep them open all the way.

"What I'm thinking," I say, "is if I'd been with you, it wouldn't have happened. We could've talked her out of it. You said she was never as wild with other people around." And then I make myself say the words that have played through my mind so many times they've become permanently engraved in my brain. "We never went to Gunning's Alley."

Molly gives me a hesitant look, like she should probably know what I'm talking about but doesn't. "What?"

"Dad never planned to take us out for pizza. The whole thing was a lie. I made it up because I was so mad at you for wanting to take Carla to the overpass."

"What?" she repeats. And then her brown eyes fly open, and she presses a hand to her throat. "Oh, Rylee."

"Yeah, stupid, right? The whole thing was so stupid," I say, and I swipe a hand over my face as my voice cracks. "I should've been with you. I'm the one who didn't stick to our pledge. Through hills and mounds, remember?"

Molly nods and closes her eyes, but not before a tear escapes and trails down the side of her nose. "I'm so sorry, Rylee...about the whole thing."

"Me too," I say. "Me too."

And then we are both crying, sitting on the steps like blubbering idiots. And when a car passes by and the driver twists her neck to stare at us, the craziness of the whole situation makes me snort. "OMG," I choke out. "We're both so pathetic."

Molly sucks in a deep breath to laugh, and the snot burbles out her nose which makes us laugh even harder. And then Coco is bouncing around, trying to lick both our faces, like she can't figure out how to handle two insane humans at once.

HAPTER SEVENTEEN

OW THAT MOLLY is back in my life, I realize how much strength and energy it took to keep her out of it. The relief is so intense it's like something alive I can touch nd hold. Not that it's all bunnies and roses between us. here's an awkwardness, a hesitation that never existed efore. It's kind of like knocking down a wall that's been 1 your way, only to discover a slippery, swinging bridge n the other side.

Still, getting ready for Dad's party is a great distraction, ecause it's hard to stress about stuff when you're blowing p balloons and licking frosting from fingers and keeping our dog from snooping through people's luggage. Our arents chase us off to bed at ten o'clock, but it's pretty bvious they are more concerned about us having time to lk than about us getting enough sleep.

And we do talk, but not about the accident. We stick to the good, safe memories—funny things we've done, school and the Wednesday Warriors. I tell her about finding Coco, and almost losing her. I even tell her about Miguel, how he's full of great writing advice, and how he's turned into a good friend. But I don't mention our clandestine spot, because I'm not sure I have the right. "Want to meet him?" I ask. "I invited him to the barbecue tomorrow."

"Oh," Molly says, followed by a really long pause. "I guess."

I can't see her expression in the dark, but the jealousy is clear in her voice, and the realization that she could actually feel threatened by one of *my* friends fills me with a giddy sense of wonder. "You'll like him," I say. "He's really nice."

"Is he cute?"

My cheeks flame, and I'm thankful she can't see. "I think so," I admit.

Molly giggles. "Okay, then," she says. "I'll check him out."

And I giggle too, because it's so good to be together again, to be fixing a connection that seemed hopelessly broken. It may never be as strong as it once was, but there's something hopeful about it, like maybe, someday, it just might be. And before I finally drift off to sleep that night, I pull Coco close and feel more peace than I have in ages.

I wake the next morning to the crinkling sound of Coco licking out an energy bar wrapper. She has a sunflower seed stuck to the top of her nose and doesn't seem to realize. Molly is a tightly curled ball in her sleeping bag, wedged between Uncle Gus's weight bench and a stack of books. I lift Coco over her and follow the bitter smell of coffee to the kitchen.

The adults are lounging on the porch, braving the cool morning in sweat pants and light jackets, looking like they plan to hang out all day. Mom catches sight of me and points to a box sitting on the wicker table. "Guess what Sharon and Chuck brought us? Doughnuts."

"Ooooh, yes," I say, pumping my fist, and everyone laughs. "Any maple bars?"

Dad shoots me a guilty look over the half eaten maple bar in his hand. "Used to be. Guess that's what you get for sleeping 'tell nine-thirty."

Chuck scratches his bald head. "Sorry, kiddo. I should've got more."

"It's okay," I say, surveying the offerings. "They're all good." I pick a chunky apple fritter and bite into its gooey sweetness. "Mmmm. Mom never buys us doughnuts."

"Best thing about the station in Elliott Bay," Dad says. "Friday morning doughnuts from the Pine Street Bakery." He glances over at Chuck. "You're still doing that, right?"

"Yes, sir," Chuck says. "There'd likely be a revolt if we stopped."

Everybody laughs again, and I study Dad's face expecting to see some trace of longing for what used to be. But his smile seems genuine, and then he starts talking about his online course, how he's decided to go for his certification in accounting. The pride in his voice makes me a little bit glad and a whole lot sad, and I don't want to hear any more of the conversation.

I go back inside and wait for Molly to get up. We watch silly YouTube videos and braid our hair before taking Coco on a long walk around the neighborhood. I show her my school, and the tree where Miguel and I rescued Oscar the kitten, and we stop for candy at Dairy Depot. By the time we get home, the Seahawks game is blaring and Uncle Gus has the chicken and pork marinating for the grill.

Mom and Karen are chopping potatoes when we walk into the kitchen, and they exchange a quick smile when they see us together. "Hey, girls," Mom says. "Want to make some biscuits for us?"

"Sure," I say, raising my eyebrows at Molly, who bobs her head in agreement.

Sharon turns from stirring something on the stove. "Oooh, I haven't had homemade biscuits in a long time."

"I've got Concord grape jelly made here in Cayuse if you want to try it," Mom says.

"Where did Brian and Rita go?" Molly asks, glancing around.

"To grab a few last things from the store," Mom says.

I know I should probably warn her before Miguel shows up out of the blue, but the thought of it makes my ears burn. Even when I follow her into the pantry to get flour, and we're alone for a few seconds, I still can't bring myself to say anything. It's just too embarrassing. Finally, I shoot him a quick text and tell him he can come over whenever he wants.

Miguel shows up about a half hour later and it's every bit as awkward as I feared. I open the door for him and do my best to act surprised. "Oh, hey, Miguel. Come on in."

His eyebrows shoot up, and he hesitates a few seconds. "You sure it's okay?" he mouths.

"It's great," I whisper back, resisting the urge to yank him inside before I change my mind. I turn to face the living room group. "This is Miguel, you guys," I announce, as casual like as possible. "We go to school together." I jab my finger around the room without meeting anyone's eyes. "You already met my Uncle Gus, and that's Sam, Chuck, and my dad."

Miguel offers a shy wave and smiles. "How's it going?"

Sam and Chuck don't know anything weird is happening, so they glance away from the game only long enough to smile and nod hello. But Dad's lips part, and his eyes bug out as he sizes up Miguel. I glance at Uncle Gus's lopsided grin and whirl away. "Come on," I tell Miguel. "Everybody else is in the kitchen."

Mom is so surprised when I introduce Miguel she drops the roll of waxed paper she's holding. But she recovers fast, swooping it up with a goofy smile. "Oh, dear, clumsy, clumsy. Nice to meet you, Miguel."

"I told him he could stay for the barbecue," I say, giving Mom a meaningful gaze. "It's okay, right?"

"Oh?" Mom says, masking her surprise with a smile. "Of course. Should be plenty."

"Thank you," Miguel says. "Smells great in here."

"Probably the biscuits Molly and I made," I say, before pointing out the slider. "She's outside with Coco. Come on, I want you to meet her."

I lead the way out to the porch and snort with laughter the second I close the door. "Sorry," I say, "crazy awkward, huh?"

Miguel cocks an eyebrow at me. "Didn't tell them I was coming, did you?"

"What! Of course I did," I say. But my giggling gives me away. "I meant to, anyway."

Coco barrels across the yard with her octopus and Miguel drops down on one knee. "Hey, Coco. How ya doing, girl?" He squints up at me. "Did you show anybody what she can do yet?"

I shake my head in warning. "Not yet," I whisper. I want to ask his advice on picking the right time, but Molly's too close so I stay quiet.

I introduce the two of them. "Hey," they both say, checking each other out with a casual glance, and I wish introducing him to the adults had been as easy. I go back inside for three glasses of orange sherbet punch, and then we hang out on the porch and talk about writing. I have Miguel retell his story about hiking with his dad and brother in the Wenatchee forest because I know Molly will think it's hilarious. She does. And as I listen to her laugh, I think how great it feels to have not only one, but two real friends.

Finally, it's time to eat, and the three of us set up lawn chairs and then help carry out the steaming platters of meat and biscuits, the bowls of corn, baked beans and coleslaw. It all smells terrific, but I'm getting more and more anxious about Coco, so the food doesn't taste near as good as it should. Coco's never performed for anyone beside Miguel and me. What if she gets stage fright and forgets everything? I'll look like a complete idiot in front of the people I care most about. But what scares me way more than Coco messing up, is Mom's reaction.

She told me if I truly wanted Dad to be happy, I'd never say anything more to him about being a fireman. That he had enough of a load to carry without us adding to it. So what will she think when she sees what I've taught Coco? Will she understand, or will she be really mad at me? And what about Dad? I want so much for him to be impressed and excited. But what if he's not? What if instead, he's simply ... hurt?

Coco meets my gaze and tips her head like she can read my mind, and for a minute I let myself believe she can. I stare back at her and try to impart how important this decision is, just how much is at stake. But after a few seconds she yawns and licks her lips, and I realize she's more interested in my chicken than in my thoughts. Oh, well. I offer her a bite and let her lick my fingers.

"How old is she?" Karen asks, and I turn to see her smiling over at me from the porch.

"I'm not sure," I say, wiping my hands on my napkin, "but I think about six months."

"She turned up as a stray at the firehouse one day," Mom explains, "and Gus brought her home while they tried to find the owner. But then he decided she was so darn cute he'd just keep her."

There's a round of bellows and roars from Chuck and Sam and Dad, and Uncle Gus holds up his hands. "Hey, now hold on, that's not how it happened."

"Aw, come on," Dad says. "Just admit it, bro, you're a pushover when it comes to cute little animals."

A shade of red colors Uncle Gus's cheeks as he laughs. "But I'm tellin' the truth. It wasn't me. Tell 'em, Rylee."

"Tell them what?" I say.

"How you conned me into keeping her."

I know he's pretty much telling the truth, but a prickle of indignation races up my spine anyway. "I did not con you," I say.

"Well, now, you promised to teach her something to help a fireman if I let you keep her, right?"

Everyone turns to me, their faces full of surprise and curiosity, and my heart nearly stops. I can't believe all the pieces have fallen into place so perfectly, without me doing a single thing. But instead of being happy, I'm terrified. "I didn't con you," I repeat, because I can't think of anything else to say.

Uncle Gus narrows his eyes at me, his expression full of challenge, and I know this is it. I will now be forced to put up or shut up. But I'm not sure I can do it. I swear the temperature has jumped twenty degrees in the last thirty seconds, and I feel like I might pass out. But then Miguel catches my eye and offers a confident smile, and it calms me just enough. I hold out my plate to Molly, who's sitting beside me. "Would you hold this for a minute?"

"Sure," she says. "What are you gonna do?"

I rise on shaky knees. "I'll show you," I say, and I pinch off a few small chunks of my biscuit. "Ready, Coco?"

She springs up and twirls with excitement, and I realize stage fright will not be a problem—not for her, anyway. I am another story. Sweat tickles its way from under my arms to my ribs, and I feel the familiar thickening in my throat. I'll probably pass out, right here in full view of everybody. But then Miguel meets my eyes again, holds his fist close to his chest and gives me a thumbs up. He at least believes in me, and it's the boost of confidence I need.

I walk halfway across the yard, Coco prancing beside me, her tail swinging and her eyes focused on the hand with the biscuit. I flash her my most assured smile. "Okay, girl, let's show them what to do in case of a fire." I raise my hand in the Stay command, back up a few feet, and then, incredibly, before I can even utter Come, Coco trots forward a few feet, lowers herself to the ground and rolls over in the most perfect stop, drop and roll she's ever done.

A couple heartbeats pass before the whole porch explodes with clapping and *Ooooohs* and *Ahhhhhs*. And it takes all I have not to burst into tears as I give Coco her bite of biscuit.

I'm too afraid to look at anyone yet, so I raise my hand and say, "Hold on," and silence settles back in. "Now we'll show you what to do if you're trapped in a smoky room." Coco watches intently as I reach down and tap the ground, then she drops to her belly and crawls after me as I back ten feet across the lawn.

"One last thing," I say, as I toss Coco her second treat. "Here's what can happen if you make the wrong choice in a fire." And I turn my thumb and forefinger into a gun, point it at Coco and she crumples to the grass.

The small group on the porch makes as much noise as the gym full of parents did at our 5th grade talent show. Someone's even stomping their feet. And I'm sure my heart will melt as I toss Coco her last bit of biscuit and gather her into my arms, whispering thanks in her silky ear. Only after that, do I finally have the courage to straighten up and face everyone.

Mom is standing behind Dad, one hand resting on his shoulder, and the other over her mouth. I can't tell for sure if she's smiling, but the corners of her eyes look crinkly, so I think she is. I know for sure Dad is. He's grinning, in fact, and then he lets out a piercing whistle that makes me feel ten feet tall. Uncle Gus is shaking his head, his face full of pride and astonishment. There's lots of smiling and clapping, and Miguel pumps his fist in victory. It all makes me so woozy with happiness I have to keep fidgeting to keep my balance.

"How in the world did you figure all that out?" Chuck asks, when the noise finally dies down.

I shrug with a smile. "YouTube," I say. And everybody laughs, like they think I'm making it up.

"Holy cow," Uncle Gus says. "I owe you an apology, Rylee. I am duly impressed."

My face burns with pride. "Thank you," I say, giving a bow. "Thank you very much. I haven't taught Coco how to bow yet, but she thanks you too."

"Wow," Dad says. "Double wow." He's looking at me like he used to, like he's seeing me again for the first time since the accident, and I bite my lip hard to keep from bawling. "You really taught her all that just so you could keep her?" Dad asks.

I bend down and pretend Coco's collar needs adjusting as I consider how to answer. The simple answer, of course, is no. I didn't do it just to keep her. I did it for *him*. And I know that right now, this precise second, is the moment I've been waiting for—my chance to explain how he can use Coco as a fire education partner. How he can still be a firefighter.

I open my mouth to begin, but then a funny thing happens—nothing. My tongue has suddenly forgotten how to do its job. But my heart hasn't. It's pounding like it's on steroids.

Mom still has a hand on Dad's shoulder, but she's lowered her other one, and she's studying me with this intense look, like she's figured it all out and is waiting to see what I decide, if I remember what she said. *Dad's firefighting days are behind him. He knows that. But he'll have a much easier time accepting it if we do.*

And I'm so torn.

But then I look at Dad again, and I think how light and happy his voice sounds when he talks about his accounting course, about his own plans for the future. And for the first time I start to understand what Mom's been trying to tell me. Maybe Dad doesn't need me to save him. Maybe he never even wanted me to. After all, he's done a pretty great job of saving himself. Maybe all he really needs from me is acceptance.

And right then is when my writer's brain makes a crazy leap from me trying to rescue Dad, to Anastar trying to rescue her mom. And I'm inspired by an amazing idea for the surprise twist I wanted. Maybe Anastar's mom doesn't need to be rescued either. Maybe she doesn't even want to be, because she's discovered the Illusionist isn't as evil as he seems. What if she's even fallen in love with him? Nobody would see that one coming! I flash Miguel a grin, because I can't wait to share my idea with him, and he offers a goofy one in return, like he has no idea what's so funny but is willing to play along anyway.

Molly's busy licking barbecue sauce from her fingers, but she catches my eye and smiles too, and I think how comforting it is to have her here. And that's when another cool thought dawns on me. Some pretty terrific things have happened recently—and none of them had anything to do with firefighting.

Dad's still studying me, still waiting for an answer to why I trained Coco. And I'm finally ready. I smile directly at him. "I wanted to see if I could train her to be a fire education dog—to help kids learn how to be safe."

Dad winks at me before raising his beer at the group sitting around him. "I think my brilliant girl may be on to something here, guys."

"Shoot yeah," Uncle Gus says. "Are you volunteering her, Rylee? Because if so, I'll let our publicity team know about her."

I nod. "Yeah, of course. But she still has to live here with me," I quickly add, just in case there's any confusion.

"Fine by me," Uncle Gus says. "As long as your mom's still okay with it."

Mom seems surprised by the comment. She bobs her head, "Oh, of course," she says.

I nod with relief, and decide that I'm more than ready to give up being the center of attention. I rub Coco's head a final time and give Mom a hopeful look. "So, is it time for cake and ice cream yet?"

CHAPTER EIGHTEEN

I T IS JUNE 12TH, *the second Saturday of summer vacation. The honeybees are buzzing, and the warm breeze smells faintly of apricots. Mom squeezes me tight as the Greyhound bus huffs up to the station. "Be safe, and have a great time," she says. "Text me as soon as you meet up with Karen and Molly."*

"I will," I promise, hugging her back. "Remind Dad to give Coco fresh water every morning, and a dog biscuit before he goes to bed."

Mom smiles. "Don't worry," she says. "Coco's in good hands."

I climb onto the bus and settle into a window seat. It's my very first trip alone, and I feel so grown up as I offer Mom a final wave before the bus roars away. I gaze out the window until we turn onto the freeway and leave Cayuse behind. Then I unzip my backpack and pull out a binder full of writing prompts and worksheets from last weekend's young author's boot camp. Pride bubbles through me as I finger the silky blue ribbon clipped to my winning chapter.

"Extraordinary," Sabrina Seoung has written in purple ink. "Well drawn characters and riveting plot. Makes me want to read the whole thing!" I'm taking it to Oregon to show Molly. But after I get home I'll hang it on my bedroom wall, just like Miguel's done with his own ribbon. Then we will begin writing about our adventure with Margo, Melanie, and Oscar in The Amazing Kitten Caper. And I think it's funny that for once I will be telling the story of someone who truly did need rescuing.

But first, I have ten whole days in Elliott Bay, and Molly and I have so much planned—shopping, bike riding, making our own soap. Most exciting, Karen has promised to take us to a salon to have professional manicures and eyebrow waxing. She claims the waxing only hurts for a few seconds, and the anticipation makes me tingle with excitement.

Then again, I've been feeling tingly ever since school let out. So maybe it's not the idea of getting my eyebrows waxed at all, but simply the promise of summer itself—opening before me like a clean, blank page, offering new beginnings and possibilities, waiting to be filled with new experiences. I'm so ready to discover what those might be. And I turn my face toward the warm sun shining through the glass and smile.

Readers!

*you enjoyed this book, would you consider taking just a
minute to write a brief review for me on Amazon.com? Just
right to the book's sale page on Amazon and click on Write
Review. It's incredibly helpful, and I'd appreciate it more
an you know! Feel free to copy and paste the same review
any other social media site you like as well. Thank you!*

anna

Check out my other middle grade novels:

A Million Ways Home
Just Left of Lucky
A Smidgen of Sky

ABOUT THE AUTHOR

Dianna Dorisi Winget has been writing since she was nine years old, when she would stuff notebooks under her bed to keep prying eyes from seeing her masterpieces. Today she's a little less shy about sharing her work. Dianna lives in the mountains of north Idaho with her husband and beagle puppy, Stella—one of many dogs she's adopted over the years from local animal shelters. She loves to hear from and respond to young readers. Find out more about Dianna and connect with her on social media.

WEBSITE:
http://diannawinget.com

GOODREADS:
http://www.goodreads.com/author/show/5573825.
Dianna_Dorisi_Winget

TWITTER:
https://Twitter.com/DiannaMWinget

INSTAGRAM:
https://www.instagram.com/dianna.writes/

Made in the USA
Monee, IL
28 April 2020